On Love

ON LOVE

aspects of a single theme

JOSÉ ORTEGA Y GASSET

translated by TOBY TALBOT

Meridian Books
THE WORLD PUBLISHING COMPANY
Cleveland and New York

Translated from the original Spanish text, ESTUDIOS
SOBRE EL AMOR.

AN ORIGINAL MERIDIAN BOOK

Published by The World Publishing Company
2231 West 110th Street, Cleveland 2, Ohio
First Meridian printing (Greenwich Editions) August 1957
Ninth Printing February, 1967
Library of Congress Catalog Card Number: 57-6688
Typography and design by Elaine Lustig
Printed in the United States of America   9 BP 267

I

features of
love

Let us begin by talking about love, but not about
"love affairs." "Love affairs" are more or less accidental episodes that happen between men and women.
Innumerable factors enter into them which compli-
cate and entangle their development to such an extent that, by and large, in most "love affairs" there is a
little of everything except that which strictly speaking deserves to be called love. A psychological analysis of "love affairs" and their picturesque casuistry is
of great interest; but we would not progress far unless we first determined what genuine love itself is.
Moreover, reducing the study of love to what men
and women feel for one another would be narrowing
the subject; indeed, Dante believed that love moves
the sun and the other planets.

Without going to these astronomical proportions, we ought to consider the phenomenon of love in its many aspects. Not only does man love woman and woman man, but we love art or science, the mother loves her child, and the religious man loves God. The immense variety and disparity of the objects into which love enters will make us cautious in considering certain attributes and qualities as integral to love which emanate instead from the diverse objects which may be loved.

For many years much has been said about love affairs and little about love. Whereas every age, since the glorious time of Greece, has had some great theory of the sentiments, the last two centuries have lacked one. The ancient world was oriented to that of Plato; subsequently to the doctrine of the Stoics. The Middle Ages assimilated that of St. Thomas and the Arabs; the seventeenth century fervently studied Descartes' and Spinoza's theories of passion. There has not been one great philosopher of the past who did not feel compelled to elaborate his own theory of the subject. We are not, however, the masters of any attempt, in the grand style, to systematize the sentiments. Only recently do the works of Pfänder and Scheler reopen the issue. In the interim, however, our inner self has become more and more complex and our perception more subtle.

The application to ourselves of older theories of the affections is clearly insufficient. The idea of love that St. Thomas gives us, in summing up Greek tradition, is, obviously, erroneous. For him, love and hate are two forms of desire, appetite, or lust. Love is the desire for something good in so far as it is good—*concupiscibile circa bonum;* hate, a negative desire, a rejection of evil as such—*concupiscibile circa malum.* This reveals the confusion between appetites or desires and sentiments from which all psychology up to the eighteenth century suffered; a confusion which we again encounter in the Renaissance, though it is transferred to the realm of esthetics. Thus, Lorenzo the Magnificent says that *l'amore è un appetito di bellezza.*

But this is one of the most important distinctions which we must make in order to prevent the very essence of love from slipping through our fingers. Nothing is so fertile in our private lives as the feeling of love; love even becomes the symbol of fertility. For many things are born out of a person's love: desire, thought, volition, action. All these things, however, which grow from love, like the harvest from a seed, are not love itself, but rather presuppose its existence. Of course, in some manner or form we also want what we love; but, on the other hand, we obviously want many things that we do not love, things which leave us indifferent on a sentimental plane. Desiring a good wine is not loving it, and the drug addict desires drugs at the same time that he hates them for their harmful effect.

There is, however, another sounder and more subtle reason for distinguishing between love and desire.

Desiring something is, without doubt, a move toward possession of that something ("possession" meaning that in some way or other the object should enter our orbit and become part of us). For this reason, desire automatically dies when it is fulfilled; it ends with satisfaction. Love, on the other hand, is eternally unsatisfied. Desire has a passive character; when I desire something, what I actually desire is that the object come to me. Being the center of gravity, I await things to fall down before me. Love, as we shall see, is the exact reverse of desire, for love is all activity. Instead of the object coming to me, it is I who go to the object and become part of it. In the act of love, the person goes out of himself. Love is perhaps the supreme activity which nature affords anyone for going out of himself toward something else. It does not gravitate toward me, but I toward it.

St. Augustine, one of those who have thought about love most profoundly and who possessed perhaps one of the most gigantic erotic temperaments that ever existed, succeeds sometimes in freeing himself from the interpretation which makes of love a desire or appetite. Thus, he says with lyric expansiveness: *Amor meus, pondus meum: illo feror, quocumque feror.* "My love is my weight; where it goes I go." Love is a gravitation toward that which is loved.

Spinoza tried to rectify this error and, side-stepping appetites, sought an emotive basis for the amorous feeling engendered by love; according to him, love must be happiness combined with knowledge of its cause; hate, on the other hand, sadness combined with knowledge of its source. Loving something or someone must consist simply in being happy and realizing, at the same time, that our happiness is produced by that something or someone. Here again we find love confused with its possible consequences. Who doubts that the lover can find happiness in his beloved? But it is no less certain that love is sometimes sad, as sad as death—a supreme and mortal torment. It is more: true love best recognizes itself and, so to speak, measures and calculates itself by the pain and suffering of which it is capable. The woman in love prefers the anguish which her beloved causes her to painless indifference. In the letters addressed by Mariana Alcoforado, the Portuguese nun, to her unfaithful seducer, one reads phrases like this: "I thank you from the bottom of my heart for the desperation you cause me, and I detest the tranquility in which I lived before I knew you."

"I clearly know what the solution to all my troubles would be. I would be free from all of them the moment I stopped loving you. But what a solution! No, I prefer suffering to forgetting you. Ah! Does this by any chance depend upon me? I cannot reproach myself for having wanted not to love you for one single moment; and finally you deserve more compassion than I, for it is better to suffer all that I suffer than to enjoy the languid pleasures that all your French lovers offer you." The first letter ends: "Goodbye; love me always and make me suffer still greater tortures." And two centuries later, Mademoiselle de Lespinasse: "I love you as one ought to love: desperately."

Spinoza did not observe carefully: loving is not happiness. He who loves his country may die for it, and the martyr may perish out of love. And conversely, there is a kind of hatred that derives pleasure from itself, that is transported with joy by the harm that befalls the hated person.

Since these famous definitions do not satisfy us, perhaps it would be better to try to describe the act of love itself, classifying it as the entomologist does an insect caught in the brush. I hope my readers now love or have loved something or someone, and can capture their feeling by its translucent wings and hold it steadily before their inner gaze. I shall enumerate the most general and abstract characteristics of that trembling bee that knows both honey and sting. The reader will judge whether or not my analysis matches what he finds within himself.

At its inception love certainly resembles desire, because its object, whether person or thing, excites it. The soul feels agitated, delicately wounded in one spot by a stimulus produced by the object. Such a stimulus has, then, a centripetal direction: it comes to us from the object. But the act of love does not begin until after that excitement, or rather, incitement. Love bursts out of the opening that the object's incisive arrow has created and actively goes toward the object: it moves hence, in the opposite direction from all incitement and desire. It goes from the lover to the beloved—from me to the other—in a centrifugal direction. This characteristic of finding oneself psychically in motion, en route *toward* an object and continually on the march from our inner being toward another is essential to love and hate. We shall soon see how the two differ. It is not simply a question of our physically moving toward the beloved, of gaining closeness and external intimacy. All of these external acts develop out of love, of course, as effects, but they do not interest us in a definition of love, and we ought to forget about them completely in our present endeavor. Everything I say refers to the act of love in its psychic inwardness as a process of the soul.

You cannot go to the God that you love with the legs of your body, and yet loving Him means going toward Him. In loving we abandon the tranquility and permanence within ourselves, and virtually migrate toward the object. And this constant state of migration is what it is to be in love.

Acts of thought or will are, you must have noticed, instantaneous. We may be rather slow in leading up to them, but their enactment does not last long: it happens in the twinkling of an eye; they are acts completed with high speed. If I understand a statement, I understand it suddenly and instantaneously. On the other hand, love is prolonged in time: one does not love in a series of sudden moments or disjointed instants which are ignited and die like the spark of a magnet, but one loves the beloved with continuity. This introduces a new note in the sentiment which we are analyzing: <u>love is a flow, a stream of spiritual matter, a fluid which flows continually like a fountain.</u> We could say, in searching for metaphoric expressions to crystallize and qualify intuitively the character of that to which I now refer, that love is not an explosion, but a continued emanation, a psychic radiation which proceeds from the lover to the beloved. It is not a single discharge, but a current.

Pfänder dwelt with great insight upon this fluid and continuous aspect of love and hate.

We have noted previously three features or traits common to love: it is centrifugal; it is a virtual going forth toward the object; and it is continuous and fluid. It is now possible to localize the fundamental difference between love and hate.

Since they are centrifugal, both love and hate move in the same direction, the person involved going toward the object; nevertheless, in spite of sharing the same direction, their reasoning and intention are different. <u>In hate, the reason being negative, one goes toward the object but against it. In love, one also goes toward the object but on its behalf.</u>

Another point that comes to our attention, as a common feature of these two sentiments and greater than their differences, is the following: thinking and wanting lack what we can call psychic temperature. Love and hate, on the other hand, compared with the thought of a mathematical theorem, have warmth and, moreover, their fire undergoes the most varied gradations. All love passes through different stages of temperature. Common language wisely speaks, therefore, of love which is cooling, and of the lover who complains of the lukewarmness or the frigidity of the beloved.

A chapter on sentimental temperature would lead us into entertaining areas of psychological observation. In such a chapter, aspects of universal history would appear which, I believe, have been overlooked by morality and art up to now. We would speak of the different temperatures of the great historic nations—the coldness of Greece, China, and of eighteenth-century Europe; the medieval ardor of romantic Europe, etc.; we would speak of the influence that the differing temperature between souls has on human relations—two human beings meet each other, and the first thing that they notice about one another is their degree of sentimental calories; in short, the quality which in artistic styles, especially literary ones, deserves to be called temperature. But it would be impossible even to scratch the surface of such a broad topic.

The degree of the temperature of love and hate is best judged if we view it from the object. What does love do on its behalf? Whether it be far or nearby, a wife or child, art or science, country or God, love exerts itself on behalf of the beloved. Desire enjoys that which is desired, derives satisfaction from it, but it offers nothing, it gives nothing, it has nothing to contribute. Love and hate are constantly active; love envelops the object in a favorable atmosphere, and whether near or far, is, in sum, endearing, flattering, affirmative, pampering. Hate envelops it, with no less passion, in an unfavorable atmosphere; it injures it, scorches it like a torrid sirocco, and virtually corrodes and destroys it. It is not necessary—I repeat—for this actually to happen; I am alluding now to the intention which goes with hate, the acts of fantasy which constitute the sentiment itself. We shall say, then, that love flows in a warm affirmation of the beloved, and hate secretes a corrosive virulence.

The opposite intention of love and hate is manifest in another form: in love we feel united with the object. What does this union mean? It is not merely physical union, or even closeness. Perhaps our friend (friendship must not be forgotten when love is generically considered) lives far away and we do not hear from him. Nevertheless, we are with him in a symbolic union—our soul seems to expand miraculously, to clear the distance, and no matter where he is, we feel that we are in essential communion with him. That is partly what we mean when, at a difficult time, we say to someone: "Count on me, for I am at your side"; that is to say, your cause is mine, and I will stick by you.

On the other hand, hate—although it is constantly

going toward what it hates—separates us from the object in the same symbolic sense. It keeps us at a radical distance and opens up an abyss. Love brings hearts together, producing harmony; hatred yields discord, metaphysical dissension, absolute isolation from the hated.

We can now begin to see the kind of activity, or, almost effort, that is involved in love and hate, in contrast to passive emotions like happiness or sadness. There is a reason for saying: to be happy or to be sad. They are, in effect, states and not efforts or acts. The sad person does nothing in regard to his sadness, nor the happy person in regard to his happiness. Love, on the other hand, reaches out to the object in a visual expansion and is involved in an invisible but divine task, the most active kind that there is: it is involved in the affirmation of its object. Think of what it is to love art or your country: it consists of never doubting for an instant their right to exist; it is like recognizing and confirming at each moment that they are worthy of existence. This, not in the manner of a judge who coldly passes a sentence in recognition of a right, but in such a way that the favorable decision is, at the same time, participation in and enactment of that right. Hating is the reverse. It is as if we were virtually killing what we hate, annihilating it in our mind, taking away its right to breathe. To hate someone is to feel irritated by his mere existence. The only thing that would bring satisfaction would be his total disappearance.

BUT NOT IN THE SENSE TO LOVE OR NOT TO LOVE — RATHER — CENTRIFUGAL FORCE ETC.

I do not think that there is a more fundamental sign of love and hate than this last one. Falling in love even once is an insistence that the beloved exists; a refusal to accept (since everything depends on that one thing) the possibility of a universe without it. But notice that this reduces itself to the *same thing,* which is to continually and intentionally give life to *something which depends upon us.* Loving is perennial vivification, creation and *intentional* preservation of what is loved. Hating is annihilation and virtual assassination—but not an assassination which is committed once, for when we hate we are constantly assassinating the hated.

If at this point we summarize the attributes of love which we have discovered, we may say that it is a centrifugal act of the soul in constant flux that goes toward the object and envelops it in warm corroboration, uniting us with it and positively affirming its being (Pfänder).

*love in
Stendhal*

1

Stendhal possessed a head full of theories; but he lacked the gifts of a theoretician. In this, as in other things, he resembles our Baroja, who reacts in an abstract way to every human problem. Both, if regarded without necessary caution, present the picture of philosophers gone astray into literature. And, yet, they are exactly the opposite. To recognize this difference it is sufficient to note that both possess an abundant collection of theories. The genuine philosopher, on the other hand, does not have more than one. This is symptomatic of the essential difference between a true theoretical temperament and a merely apparent one.

The theoretician arrives at a philosophic conclusion due to an exasperated desire to concur with reality. With this end in mind, he takes infinite precautions, one of which is to maintain the multitude of his ideas in strict unity and cohesion. He is aware that what is real is remarkably singular. What terror Parmenides felt when he discovered this! In contrast to the real, our minds and our sensibilities are disjointed, contradictory and multiform. In Stendhal and in Baroja, philosophic conclusions descend to mere language, to a literary genre which serves as an instrument for literary outburst. They think in terms of "for" and "against"—and this the thinker never does. In effect, they love and hate conceptually. Therefore, their theories are numerous. They swarm about like bacteria, disparate and antagonistic, each one engendered by the impression of the moment. In the manner of songs they tell a truth, not about things, but about the singer.

I do not mean to insinuate any criticism by this. Neither Stendhal nor Baroja particularly aspired to be numbered among the philosophers; and if I have pointed out this indecisive aspect of their intellectual nature, it has been only for the delight of taking people as they are. They seem to be philosophers. *Tant pis!* But they aren't. *Tant mieux!*

Stendhal's case is, however, more difficult than that of Baroja, because there is one subject upon which he tried to theorize in complete seriousness. And it is, by coincidence, the same subject which Socrates, the patron of philosophers, thought to be his own specialty. *Ta erotika:* the question of love.

The study *De l'amour* is one of the most widely read of books. We arrive in the sitting-room of a marquise, an actress, or simply a cosmopolitan lady. We have to wait a few moments. The pictures—why are there inevitably pictures on the wall?—are the first to capture our attention. There is no escaping it; moreover, the pictures always produce in us the same impression of whim. The picture is what it is; but it could just as easily have been otherwise. We always miss that dramatic emotion of coming upon a necessary thing. Then comes the furniture, and with it some books. A book jacket. What does it say? *De l'amour.* It is like a work on diseases of the liver in a doctor's office. The marquise, the actress, the cosmopolitan lady, indefatigably long to be specialists in love; they want to become informed, just as someone who buys an automobile receives a complimentary manual on combustion engines.

The book makes delightful reading. Stendhal always tells a story, even when he is defining, reasoning, and theorizing. He is, for me, the best narrator there is, the supreme narrator before the Almighty. But is his famous theory defining love as crystallization true? Why hasn't a thorough study been made of it? It has been toyed with, but no one has subjected it to an adequate analysis. Didn't it deserve the effort?

Note that, in sum, this theory defines love as an essential fiction. It is not that love sometimes makes

STENDAHL'S THEORY

mistakes, but that it is, essentially, a mistake. We fall in love when our imagination projects non-existent perfections onto another person. One day the phantasmagoria vanishes, and with it love dies. This is worse than declaring, as of yesteryear, that love is blind. For Stendhal it is less than blind: it is imaginary. Not only does it not see what is real, but it supplants the real.

All anyone has to do is to study this theory on the surface to be able to situate it in time and space: it is a typical product of nineteenth-century Europe. It bears the characteristic features: idealism and pessimism. The theory of "crystallization" is idealistic because it makes the external object for which we live a mere projection of the individual. Since the Renaissance, the European leans toward this manner of explaining the world as a manifestation of the spirit. Up to the nineteenth century this idealism was relatively cheerful. The world which the individual projects about him is, in its own way, real, genuine, and meaningful. But the theory of "crystallization" is pessimistic. It tries to show that what we consider normal functions of our spirit are nothing more than special cases of abnormality. Thus, Taine wishes to convince us that normal perception is merely a continuous, connected hallucination. This is typical of the ideology of the past century. The normal is explained by the abnormal, the superior by the inferior. There is a strange persistence in the view that the Universe is an absolute *quid pro quo*, essentially nonsense. The moralist will try to insinuate that all altruism is masked egotism. Darwin will patiently describe the constructive service that death performs to life, and he will make the struggle for existence the prime vital force. Similarly, Karl Marx will place the class struggle at the root of history.

But the truth is so contrary to this harsh pessimism that it manages to slip in, unnoticed by the bitter thinker. So it is with the theory of "crystallization"; because finally one recognizes in it that a man loves only what is lovable, what is worthy of being loved. But not possessing it—so it seems—in reality, he is compelled to imagine it. These fantasized perfections are what elicit love. It is very easy to label fine things illusory. But whoever does this forgets to face the problem that then results. If these fine things do not exist, how did they come to our attention? If there are not sufficient real reasons in the woman for inspiring amorous exaltation, then at what non-existent *ville d'eaux* could we have met the imaginary woman thus capable of exciting us?

The influence of fraudulence in love is obviously exaggerated. When we notice that qualities are sometimes invented which, in reality, the loved one does not possess, we should ask ourselves if it is not the love itself which is falsified. A psychology of love must be very suspicious of the genuineness of the sentiment it is analyzing. To my mind, the most trenchant element in Stendhal's treatise is this suspicion that there are cases of love that are not really love.

His famous classification of erotic categories—*amour-goût, amour-vanité, amour passion,* et cetera—bears out his suspicion of such spurious cases. It is quite natural that if a love affair begins by being false in regard to love itself everything else about it will likewise be false, especially the object that inspires it.

Only "passion-love" is legitimate for Stendhal. I think, however, that even this term does not sufficiently reduce the circle of true love. In "passion-love" as well, different categories should be introduced. Love is not only invented out of vanity or *goût.* There is another more direct and persistent source of falsification. Love is the most highly eulogized activity. Poets have always embellished and refined it with their cosmetic instruments, endowing it with a strange abstract reality, to such a point that before experiencing it we know all about it, place high value on it, and are resolved to practice it, like an art or profession. Well, then: imagine a man or woman who abstractedly makes love, *in genere,* the ideal of his or her vital action. Such beings will live in a constant state of fictitious love. They needn't wait for a particular object to excite their erotic streak, for anyone will serve the purpose. They love love, and *what* is loved is nothing more, strictly speaking, than a pretext. A man to whom this happens, if he has a taste for thought, will infallibly invent the theory of crystallization.

Stendhal is one of these lovers of love. In his recent

book on *The Amorous Life of Stendhal*, Abel Bonnard writes: "All he asks of women is that they sub-
stantiate his illusions. He loves so as not to feel
lonely; but, in truth, he alone invents three-quarters
of his love affairs."

There are two kinds of doctrines of love. One of
them contains the conventional theories, sheer topics,
which are reiterated without any intuition into the
realities which they expound. The other consists of
more substantial notions, which derive from personal
experience. Thus, our abstract thoughts about love
give a picture of our love affairs.

In Stendhal's case there isn't any doubt. We are
dealing with a man who never truly loved nor, above
all, was ever truly loved. His life is filled with false
love affairs. All that false love affairs can leave in
one's soul is the melancholy knowledge of their own
falseness and the experience of their dissolution. If
you break down and analyze the Stendhalian theory,
you clearly see that it was thought out backwards;
I mean that, for Stendhal, the culminating fact in
love is its termination. How can one explain the fact
that love comes to an end, if indeed the beloved object remains unchanged? Rather would it be more
exact to suppose—as Kant did in his theory of knowledge—that our erotic emotions are not controlled by
the object toward which they move, but, on the contrary, that the object is conceived by our impassioned
fantasy? Love dies because its birth was an error.

Chateaubriand would not have thought this, because his experience was quite the contrary. Here is a man who—incapable of truly feeling love—had the gift of truly inspiring it. One woman after another on coming in contact with him was suddenly smitten by love forever. *Suddenly and forever.* Chateaubriand, of necessity, would have outlined a doctrine whereby it would be essential for true love to be born suddenly and never to die.

2

Comparing the love affairs of Chateaubriand and Stendhal yields psychologically rich material for teaching a few things to those who speak of Don Juan so lightly. Here are two men with gigantic creative powers. One cannot say that they are merely inconsequential effeminate fellows—a ridiculous image to which Don Juan has been reduced by certain narrow, shallow minds. Both men devoted their greatest energy to the endeavor of being uninterruptedly in love. Clearly, they did not succeed. Apparently, it is a difficult matter for an elevated spirit to succumb to an amorous passion. But the point is that day after day they tried, almost always successfully, to create for themselves the illusion that they were in love. They took their love affairs much more seriously than their work. It is curious that only those incapable of producing great work believe that the contrary is the proper conduct: to take science, art, or politics seriously and disdain love affairs as mere frivolities. I don't take sides: I wish only to point out that the great productive human beings have usually been people who were not very serious, according to the *petit-bourgeois* conception of that virtue.

But the interesting thing from the Don Juan point of view is the contrast between Stendhal and Chateaubriand. Of the two, Stendhal is the one who exerts himself most arduously on behalf of women. However, he is exactly the opposite of Don Juan. The true Don Juan, unlike Stendhal, is quite different: always removed from the woman and wrapped in his cloak of melancholy, he is, more than likely, never moved to woo any woman at all.

The greatest error that one can commit when he is trying to define the figure of Don Juan is to focus his attention on men who spend their lives making love to women. At best such a focus will yield a trivial and inferior type of Don Juan. More probably, however, it will produce, instead of Don Juan, an exactly opposite type. It is precisely because the bad poet is not a poet that we find in him only the anxiety, tumult, sweat, and effort with which he vainly aspires to what he cannot achieve. The bad poet substitutes for the missing inspiration the conventional trappings: long hair and flowing tie. In the same way, the dauntless Don Juan who each day performs his stint of eroticism, this Don Juan who so clearly "resembles" Don Juan, is exactly his negation and his vacuum.

Don Juan is not the man who makes love to women, but the man to whom women make love.

This, indeed, is the indisputable human fact to which those writers, who have recently introduced the serious theme of *Donjuanism*, should have given more thought. It is a fact that there are men with whom women fall in love with astounding intensity and frequency. Here is, indeed, something to consider. Of what does this strange gift consist? What vital mystery is hidden behind this privilege? Following the other procedure, that of moralizing about any ridiculous figure who passes himself off as a Don Juan, seems to me too naive to be fruitful. It is the eternal vice of preachers: to invent a stupid Manichaean for the purpose of having the pleasure of refuting the Manichaean.

Stendhal devotes forty years to overcoming feminine defenses. He arduously constructs a strategic system, replete with principles and corallaries. He tenaciously works at the problem, persists and exhausts himself in the task. The result is nil. Stendhal never succeeded in being truly loved by any woman. This should not be very surprising. Most men suffer the same fate. To compensate somewhat for this misfortune the custom and illusion has been created of accepting a certain vague attachment or tolerance for a woman as true love, and this, achieved by dint of a thousand efforts. The same thing is true here as in the realm of aesthetics. Most men die without ever having enjoyed from art a genuine emotion. Nevertheless, it has been agreed to accept as valid substitutes the flutter that a waltz produces or the dramatic interest that a well-publicized novel agitates.

Stendhal's loves were pseudo-loves of this class. Abel Bonnard appropriately does not stress this in *The Amorous Life of Stendhal,* which I have just read and which prompts me to write these notes. This point is important because it explains the fundamental error in his theory of love. The basis of the error is a false experience.

Stendhal believes—as a result of the facts of his experience—that love "is made" and, moreover, that it ends. Both attributes are characteristic of pseudo-loves.

Chateaubriand, on the contrary, always finds love "made." He does not have to work at it. The woman passes alongside him and suddenly feels charged with a magic electricity. She surrenders immediately and totally. Why? Ah! That is the secret that writers on *Donjuanism* should have revealed to us. Chateaubriand is not a handsome man. Small and stooped. Always ill-tempered, disagreeable, and detached. His attachment to his love lasts for a week. However, any woman who fell in love with him at twenty continued at eighty to be bound to this "genius," whom perhaps she never saw again. These are not figments of the imagination: they are documented facts.

One example among many: the Marquise de Custine, the "first lady" of France. She belonged to one of the noblest familes and was extremely beautiful.

During the revolution, while practically a child, she is condemned to the guillotine. She is saved, thanks to the love which she arouses in a shoemaker, a member of the Tribunal. She emigrates to England. When she returns, Chateaubriand has just published *Atala*. She meets the author, and a mad passion immediately erupts within her. Chateaubriand, forever capricious, gets the idea that Madame de Custine ought to buy the Fervaques castle, an ancient manorial residence where Henry IV spent a night. The Marquise gathers all that she can of her fortune, which is still not properly restored since the emigration, and buys the castle. But Chateaubriand is in no hurry to visit it. Finally, after some time, he spends a few days there, sublime hours for that impassioned woman. Chateaubriand reads a couplet which Henry IV installed in the fireplace with his hunting knife:

> *La dame de Fervaques*
> *mérite de vives ataques.*

The hours of bliss slip quickly by, never to be recaptured. Chateaubriand leaves, never to return; he is already bound for new islands of love. The months and years go by. The Marquise de Custine is approaching seventy. One day she shows the castle to a visitor. When the latter reaches the room with the fireplace, he says: "So this is the place where Chateaubriand was at your feet?" And she, quickly, astonished and seemingly offended: "Oh, no, sir; I at Chateaubriand's feet!"

ANSWER

This kind of love in which a human being remains attached once and for all to another being—a sort of metaphysical grafting—was unknown to Stendhal. He believes, therefore, that it is essential that love consume itself, when probably the contrary is closer to the truth. A love which has sprung from the roots of a person in all likelihood cannot die. It is forever grafted to the sensitive soul. Circumstance—for example, distance—can prevent its necessary nourishment, in which case the love will lose its force, will change into a sentimental wisp, a slight vein of emotion which will continue to pulsate in the subsoil of consciousness. But it will not die: its sentimental quality will remain intact. In his innermost depth the person who has once loved continues to feel that he is part of his beloved. Chance may take her elsewhere in physical and social space, but that does not matter, for she will continue to be close to the one she loves. This is the supreme sign of true love: being close to what is loved, in a more profound contact and proximity than that of space. It means being with the other vitally. The most exact, but too technical, phrase would be this: an ontological state of being with the beloved, faithful to its destiny, no matter what it is. The woman who loves the thief, regardless of where her body may be, is with her senses in jail.

3

Stendhal derives the name "crystallization," which he gives to his theory of love, from a well-known phenomenon. If you throw a branch from a shrub into the Salzburg mines and retrieve it the following day, it appears transformed. The humble botanical form has been covered with iridescent crystals which exquisitely embroider its surface. According to Stendhal, a similar process occurs in a soul capable of love. The real likeness of a woman penetrates the masculine soul, and little by little becomes embroidered with imagined superstructures, which act to heap upon the bare likeness every possible perfection.

I have always believed this famous theory to be completely false. Perhaps the only thing we can salvage from it is the implicit—though unstated—recognition that love, in some way, is a striving for perfection. Stendhal finds it necessary to assume in his theory of "crystallization" that we imagine these imputed perfections. He is not, however, concerned with this point; he takes it for granted, relegates it to the background of his theory, and does not even bother to observe that it is not the most grave, profound, and mysterious moment of love. The theory of "crystallization" concerns itself rather with explaining the failure of love, the disillusion of unfulfilled ardor; in sum, the act of falling out of love, rather than the act of falling in love.

Like a good Frenchman, Stendhal is superficial from the very moment that he begins to speak in generalizations. He goes directly past the essential and formidable fact without noticing it, or feeling any surprise. But, then, feeling surprised at what seems most natural and evident is the philosopher's talent. Observe how Plato unwaveringly goes straight to the point and grasps the awesome nerve of love with his intellectual pincers. "Love," he says, "is a desire for generation and birth in beauty." "What naiveté!" say the lady experts on love, while drinking their cocktails in all the Ritz hotels of the world. The ladies do not suspect the philosopher's ironic complacency when he beholds that his words make their enchanting eyes flash with this accusation of naiveté. They forget perhaps that when a philosopher speaks to them about love he is not making love to them. Quite the contrary; in fact, as Fichte pointed out, philosophizing means precisely not living, and living means precisely not philosophizing. What a delightful ability the philosopher possesses of detaching himself from life; he has a virtual capacity to escape life, a capacity which he clearly perceives, while to a woman he appears merely naive! Like Stendhal, the only things that interest a lady in the doctrine of love are its superficial psychology and anecdotes. I do not deny that these are interesting; all I wish to insinuate is that behind all this are greater problems, that of eroticism, and the supreme one, which Plato formulated twenty-four centuries ago.

Though only obliquely, let us examine this supreme problem for a moment.

In Platonic vocabulary, "beauty" is the concrete name for what, more generically, we call "perfection." Worded with some caution, but hewing strictly to Plato's intention, his idea is this: inherent in all love is a desire of the one in love to unite with another being who appears endowed with a certain perfection. It is, then, a movement of our souls toward something which, in some way, is outstanding, better than average, superior. Whether this superiority is real or imaginary does not in the least alter the fact that erotic feeling—or, to put it more exactly, sexual love—is only produced when we are confronted with something which we judge to be perfect. Let the reader try to imagine a state of love—of sexual love—in which the object is totally lacking in any trace of excellence in the eyes of the one in love, and he will see how impossible it is. Let us say, for the time being, that falling in love consists in feeling oneself enchanted by something (we shall soon see in some detail what this matter of "enchantment" is), and this something can cause enchantment only if it is or seems to be perfect. I do not mean that the loved one seems to be completely perfect—that is the error Stendhal makes. It is enough if there is some perfection in him, for clearly perfection on the human plane does not mean something which is absolutely good, but rather something which is better than the rest, some quality which, by virtue of the relationship, stands out; in short, superiority.

This is the first thing. Secondly, it is this superiority which stirs one to seek union with the person who possesses it. What is this "union"? The most genuine

lovers will truthfully admit that they did not feel—
at least, initially—a desire for physical union. This
point is delicate and requires the greatest precision.
It does not mean that the lover does not also want
bodily union with his beloved. But for the very reason
that he wants that "also," it would be false to say that
that is all he wants.

An important consideration is called for here. No
one has ever made a clear distinction—perhaps with
the sole exception of Scheler—between "sexual love"
and the "sexual instinct." Their confusion is such
that when the first is mentioned it is generally understood to be the second. Of course, in man, instincts
almost always appear linked with superinstinctual
forms of a mental and even spiritual character. We
very rarely see a pure instinct functioning separately.
The customary idea of "physical love" is, in my opinion, exaggerated. It is neither frequent nor easy to
feel physical attraction exclusively. In the great
majority of cases, sexuality is supported and complicated by germs of sentimental ardor, of admiration
for physical beauty, sympathy, etc. Nevertheless,
cases of purely instinctive sexual practice are numerous enough to be distinguishable from true "sexual
love." The difference seems clear, especially in the
two extreme situations: when the practice of sexuality
is repressed because of moral reasons or circumstance, or when, on the contrary, its excess degenerates into lust. In both cases one notes that "as distinguished from love" pure voluptuousness—we could

say pure impurity—exists prior to its object. One feels desire before knowing the person or situation which satisfies it. Consequently, anyone is able to satisfy it. Instinct does not show preferences when it is mere instinct. It is not, by itself, an impulse toward any perfection.

The sexual instinct assures, perhaps, conservation of the species, but not its perfection. On the other hand, genuine sexual love, that is, ardor for another being, his body and soul in indissoluble union, is in itself primarily a gigantic force entrusted with improving the species. Instead of existing prior to its object, it is always born in response to a being who appears before us, and who, by virtue of some eminent quality which he possesses, stimulates the erotic process.

Scarcely does this begin, than the lover experiences a strange urgency to dissolve his own individuality in that of the other and, vice versa, to absorb the individuality of his beloved into his own. A mysterious longing! Whereas in every other situation in life nothing upsets us so much as to see the frontiers of our individual existence trespassed upon by another person, the rapture of love consists in feeling ourselves so metaphysically porous to another person that only in the fusion of both, only in an "individuality of two," can it find fulfillment. This view recalls the doctrine of the Saint-Simonians, according to which authentic individuality consists in the unity formed of man and woman. However, the longing for fusion does not end with simple, uncreative union. Love is complete when it culminates in a more or less clear desire to leave, as testimony of the union, a child in whom the perfections of the beloved are perpetuated and affirmed. This third element, precipitated by love, seems to sum up its essential meaning in all its purity. The child is neither the father's nor the mother's: he is the personified union of the two and is a striving for perfection modeled after flesh and soul. Naïve Plato was right: love is a desire to generate in perfection or, as another Platonist, Lorenzo de Medici, was to say: *es appetito di belleza.*

The ideology of recent times has lost cosmological inspiration and has become almost exclusively psychological. Refinements in the psychology of love, by multiplying subtle casuistry, have drawn away our attention from this cosmic dimension, which is elemental to love. We too are about to enter the psychological zone, although attacking what is most essential to it. We must not forget, however, that the multiform history of our loves, with all their complications and incidents, lives finally from that elemental, cosmic force, which our psyche—primitive or refined, simple or complex, from one century to another— merely administers and models in varied ways. The differently styled turbines and engines which we submerge in the torrent should not make us forget that it is the primary force of the torrent itself which mysteriously moves us.

4

There is an undeniable and evident germ of truth in
the theory of "crystallization." It is a fact that we are
frequently faced with a mistake in the course of our
loves. We imagined non-existent charms and skills in
the beloved. Ought we not then to agree with Stendhal? I think not. It is possible to be wrong as a result
of being too right. It would be outlandish to conclude
that, after being consistently wrong in our dealings
with reality, we should hit the mark in love alone.
The projection of imaginary qualities upon a real object is a constant phenomenon. In man, to see things
—moreover, to appreciate them!—always means to
complete them. Even Descartes noticed that when he
opened the window and thought he saw men passing
in the street, he was not being exact. What was it
that he really saw?—*chapeaux et manteaux: rien de
plus.* (A curious impressionistic painter's observation
which makes us think of Velazquez' *Les petits che-
valiers,* kept in the Louvre and copied by Manet.)
Strictly speaking, no one sees things in their naked
reality. The day this happens will be the last day of
the world, the day of the great revelation. In the
meantime, let us consider our perception of reality
which, in the midst of a fantastic fog, allows us at
least to capture the skeleton of the world, its great
tectonic lines, as adequate. Many, in fact the majority, do not even achieve this: they live from words
and suggestions; they lead a somnambulent existence,

scurrying along in their delirium. What we call genius is only the magnificent power which some men
possess of piercing a portion of that imaginative fog
and discovering beyond it a new authentic bit of reality, quivering in sheer nakedness.

That which appears to be evident, therefore, in the
theory of "crystallization" extends beyond the problem of love. All of our mental life is, in varying degrees, a crystallization. It is not, then, something
pertaining specifically to the case of love. All that we
can assume is that in the erotic process crystallization
increases in abnormal proportions. This, however, is
completely false in the sense which Stendhal assumes. The lover's valuation is no more illusory than
that of the political partisan, the artist, the business
man, etc. One is more or less as perspicacious or ob-
tuse in love as he ordinarily is in judging his fellow
beings. Most people are dull in their perception of
people, for people are the most complicated and elusive objects in the universe.

All that one has to do to shatter the theory of crystallization is to examine the cases in which it evi-
dently does not appear: they are the exemplary cases
of love in which both parties possess a clear mind
and, within human limits, are not liable to be mistaken. A theory of eroticism ought to begin by an explanation of its most perfect forms, and not by an
immediate orientation toward the pathology of the
phenomenon which it is studying. The fact is that,
in those cases, the man, rather than projecting perfec-

tions which existed only in his mind, suddenly discovers in a woman certain qualities of a nature which
until then were unrecognized by him. Note that these
are specifically feminine qualities. If they are at all
prototypic, how can they pre-exist in the mind of the
male? Or, vice versa, how can masculine virtues be
anticipated by a feminine mind? The element of truth
which there may be in a possible anticipation and, as
it were, invention of charms before they are found in
reality, has nothing to do with Stendhal's idea. We
shall presently consider this elusive matter.

There is in this theory, first of all, considerable
error in observation. It seems to assume that the state
of love implies a super-activity of the consciousness.
Stendhalian crystallization seems to indicate a super-
abundance of spiritual effort, enrichment and cir-
cumlocution. On the contrary, however, falling in
love is a state of mental misery which has a restricting, impoverishing, and paralyzing effect upon the
development of our consciousness.

I said "falling in love." To avoid uttering the
usual nonsense on the subject of love, it is necessary
to be rather strict about our vocabulary. The word
"love," so simple and with so few letters, is used to
label innumerable phenomena which differ so widely
that it would be well to doubt if they have anything in
common with each other. We speak of "love for a
woman"; but also of "love of God," "love of country,"
"love of art," "maternal love," "filial love," etc. One

and the same word embraces and names the most varied fauna of emotions.

A term is equivocal when we designate things with it which do not have some essential common feature, an important aspect which is identical in all of them. So with the word "lion," [1] used to name the famous feline at the same time as it is employed to designate the Roman Popes and the Spanish city of León. Chance is responsible for making one phoneme bear different meanings, which refer to and designate radically different objects. Grammarians and logicians speak then of "polysemia": words which possess multiple meanings.

Is this the case of the name "love" in the aforementioned expressions? Is there some important similarity which exists between "love for a woman" and "love of science"? When we examine both states of mind we find that almost every element in them differs. There is, however, one identical ingredient, which a careful analysis would enable us to isolate in both phenomena. If we saw it freed and isolated from the remaining factors which make up both states of mind, we would understand that, strictly speaking, it alone deserves the name of "love." By virtue of a practical but inaccurate amplification, we apply the name to the entire state of mind in spite of the fact that many things are involved in the lat-

[1] *León* in Spanish (Translator).

ter which are not really "love," or even sentiment.

It is lamentable that psychological research of the past hundred years has not yet flowed into the general cultural stream, and it is still generally necessary to resort to thick lenses, commonly used to view the human psyche.

Love, strictly speaking,[2] is pure sentimental activity toward an object, which can be anything—person or thing. As a "sentimental" activity, it remains, on the one hand, separated from all intellectual functions—perception, consideration, thought, recall, imagination—and, on the other hand, from desire, with which it is often confused. A glass of water is desired, but is not loved, when one is thirsty. Undoubtedly, desires are born of love; but love itself is not desire. We desire good fortune for our country, and we desire to live in it because we love it. Our love exists prior to these desires, and the desires spring from love like the plant from the seed.

As with all sentimental "activity," love is different from inactive sentiments, such as joy or sadness. The latter are a sort of coloration which tinges the human being. One "is" sad or he "is" happy, in complete passiveness. Joy, in itself, does not constitute any action, although it may lead to it. On the other hand, loving something is not simply "being," but acting toward that which is loved. In this regard

[2] That is, love alone and not the total state of the person in love.

I am not referring to the physical or spiritual movements which love incites; love itself is, by nature, a transitive act in which we exert ourselves on behalf of what we love. Although we are quiescent, when we are a hundred leagues from the object and not even thinking about it, if we love the object an indefinable flow of a warm and affirmative nature will emanate from us. This is clearly observable if we compare love with hate. To hate something or someone is not "being" passive, like being sad, but, in some way, it is a terrible negative action, ideally destructive of the hated object. This observation that there is a specific sentimental activity, which is distinct from all physical and spiritual activities, such as those of the intellect, desire, and volition, seems to me of a crucial importance for a refined psychology of love. When love is spoken about, there is almost always a description of its consequences or concomitances, its driving motives or its results. Love itself is scarcely ever seized by the analytical pincers, with respect to its peculiarities and differences from the rest of the psychic fauna.

It may now appear admissible that "love of science" and "love for a woman" have a common denominator. Sentimental activity, that is, a cordial, affirmative interest in another person for himself, can equally be directed toward a woman, a piece of land (one's country), a branch of human activity such as sports, science, etc. Moreover, one might add, leaving aside pure sentimental activity, that all the differing elements in "love of science" and "love of a woman" are not, properly speaking, what love is.

There are many "cases of love" in which there is a bit of everything except love. There is desire, curiosity, persistence, madness, sincere sentimental fiction; but there is no intense affirmation of another being, irrespective of his attitude toward us. As for the "cases of love" where we really find this affirmation, we must not forget that they contain, *sensu stricto,* many other elements besides love.

In a broad sense, we usually consider love to be what is in fact only the "act of falling in love," a highly complex state of mind in which love in the strict sense has a secondary role. Stendhal refers to this state when he titles (with an abusive generality which reveals the inadequacy of his philosophic horizon) his book, *De l'amour.*

In regard to this "falling in love" which the theory of crystallization presents to us as a hyperactivity of the mind, I should like to say that it is, rather, a contraction and a relative paralysis of the life of our consciousness. Under its sway, we are below, and not above, the par of our normal existence. This leads us into an analysis of the pattern of the psychology of the erotic seizure.

5

"Falling in love" is a phenomenon of attention.

No matter at what moment we examine the life of our consciousness, we will find its field engaged by a multitude of external and internal objects. These objects, which in each case fill the capacity of our minds, do not form a disorderly array. There is always a minimal order in them, an hierarchy. In fact, we always find that one of them stands out apart from the others, perferred and especially illuminated, as if our mental focus, our preoccupation, might tone down its radiance by isolating it from the rest. It is natural for our consciousness to focus on something. But it is impossible for it to focus on something without disregarding other things which remain thereby as a secondary presence, in the manner of a chorus or a background.

Since the number of objects which compose the world of each of us is very large and the field of our consciousness very limited, there exists among them a sort of struggle to gain our attention. Properly speaking, our spiritual and mental life is merely that which takes place in the zone of maximum illumination. The rest—the zone of conscious inattention and, beyond that, the subconscious—is only potential life, a preparation, an arsenal or reserve. The attentive consciousness can be regarded as the very space of our personalities. We can just as well say that we are attentive to a thing as say that that thing dislodges a certain space in our personalities.

In the normal course, the focus of attention occupies this privileged center for a few moments and is soon driven out to leave its place to something else. To sum up, attention shifts from one object to another, remaining briefly or at length fixed upon each in accordance with its vital importance. Imagine what would happen if one fine day our attention became paralyzed, fixed upon one object. The rest of the world would be banished, removed, as though non-existent, and, lacking every possible comparison, the object of our abnormal attention would acquire enormous proportions for us. So much so that it would actually occupy the entire gamut of our minds and alone would be equivalent for us to that whole world which, thanks to our radical inattention, we left behind. The same thing happens, therefore, as when we bring our hand up to our eyes; though it is so small a body, it is enough to blot out the rest of the landscape and to fill our entire field of vision. What we fix our attention upon has for us *ipso facto* greater reality, a more vigorous existence than what we do not focus upon, an anemic and almost phantasmic background which lurks on the periphery of our minds. Since it has greater reality, it of course achieves greater esteem, merit, and importance and compensates for the obscured remainder of the universe.

When attention is fixed upon an object for a greater length of time or with greater frequency than normal, we speak about "mania." The maniac is a man with an abnormal attention-span. Almost all great men have been maniacs, except that the consequences of their mania, of their "fixed idea," seem useful or commendable to us. When Newton was asked how he had been able to discover his mechanical system of the universe, he answered: *Nocte dieque incubando* (By thinking about it day and night). This is a declaration of obsession. In truth, nothing characterizes us as much as our field of attention. It is differently modulated in every man. Thus, for the man given to contemplation, who follows every subject through to make it yield its innermost substance, the lightness with which the worldly man's attention skips from object to object is a cause of vexation. Conversely, the man of the world is wearied and distressed by the slowness with which the thinker's attention advances, moving as it does like a dragnet scratching the rough bottom of an abyss. Moreover, there are different preferences of attention which constitute the very basis of character. There are those who, if a fact of economics comes up in conversation, react as violently as if they had mentally fallen through a trap door. Another's attention will spontaneously descend toward art or sexual matters. This formula might well be accepted: tell me where your attention lies and I will tell you who you are.

I believe that "falling in love" is a phenomenon of attention, but of an abnormal state of attention which occurs in a normal man.

The initial stage of "falling in love" immediately reveals this. In society many men and women are confronted with each other. The attention of each man—as of each woman—shifts indifferently from one representative of the opposite sex to another. Reasons based on former sentimental ties, greater proximity, etc., will cause the woman's attention to rest a bit longer upon one male than upon another; but the disproportion between attention to one and inattention to the rest is not great. To put it another way—and barring slight differences—every man that a woman knows is equi-distant from her attention, in one straight line. One day, however, this equal division of attention ceases. The woman's attention of itself seems to rest upon one of those men, and soon it requires an effort for her to dismiss him from her thoughts, to mobilize her preoccupation toward other things. The straight line has been broken: one man stands out at a closer distance to the woman's attenion.

"Falling in love," initially, is no more than this: attention abnormally fastened upon another person. If the latter knows how to utilize his privileged situation and ingeniously nourishes that attention, the rest follows with irremissible mechanism. Each day he will find himself further advanced before the line of those others, the indifferent ones; each day he will occupy more space in the mind of the attentive woman. She will begin to feel incapable of ignoring the privileged man. Other people and things will gradually be dislodged from her consciousness. Wherever "the woman in love," whatever her apparent occupation, her attention will gravitate by its own weight toward that man. And, vice versa, it will require a great effort on her part to tear her attention away from that direction for one moment and orient it toward life's obligations. St. Augustine wisely observed this spontaneous absorption in an object which is characteristic of love: *Amor meus, pondus meum: illo feror, quocumque feror.* (My love is my weight: because of it I move.)

It is not a question, then, of an enrichment of our mental lives. Quite the contrary. There is a progressive elimination of the things which formerly absorbed us. Consciousness contracts and is occupied by only one object. The attention remains paralyzed: it does not advance from one thing to another. It is fixed and rigid, the captive of one person alone. *Theia manía* (divine mania), said Plato. (We shall soon see where this surprising and excessive "divine" comes from.)

Nevertheless, the person in love has the impression that the life of his consciousness is very rich. His reduced world is more concentrated. All of his psychic forces converge to act upon one single point, and this gives a false aspect of superlative intensity to his existence.

At the same time, that exclusiveness of attention endows the favored object with portentous qualities. It is not that non-existent perfections are imagined in it. (I have already shown that this can happen; but it is neither essential nor necessary, as Stendhal erroneously supposes.) By overwhelming an object with attention and concentrating on it, the consciousness endows it with an incomparable force of reality. It exists for us at every moment; it is ever present, there alongside us, more real than anything else. The remainder of the world must be sought out, by laboriously deflecting our attention from the beloved.

Here is where we encounter a great similarity between falling in love and mystical ardor. The mystic frequently speaks of "the presence of God." It is not merely an expression. Behind it lies an authentic phenomenon. Through prayer, meditation, and addressing God, the latter acquires such objective solidity for the mystic that it is never permitted to vanish from the range of his thoughts. It is always there, precisely because attention does not let go of it. Every activity of the mystic's day brings him into contact with God, that is, makes him revert to his idea. This is not something peculiar to religious orders. There is nothing that can attain that everlasting presence which, according to the mystic, God enjoys. The sage who spends years at a time thinking about a problem and the novelist who is constantly harrowed by preoccupation with his imaginary character share the same phenomenon. And so Balzac winds up a business conversation by saying: "Well, let us return to reality! Let us talk about César Birotteau." For the lover his beloved also possesses a constant presence. It is as if the entire world is compressed in her. Actually, what happens is that the world does not exist for the lover. His beloved has dislodged and replaced it. That is why the lover in an Irish song says: "My darling, you are my share of the world!"

6

Romantic poses aside, let us recognize that "falling in love"—I repeat that I am not talking about love *sensu stricto*—is an inferior state of mind, a form of transitory imbecility. Without a paralysis of con-

...ction of our habitual world, we

...ove.

...f "love" is, as you see, the re-

...by Stendhal. Instead of heaping

...ctions) upon an object, as the

...ion presumes, what we do is to

...an abnormal degree and remain

...nd paralyzed, like a rooster be-

...e line.

...ean to disparage the great erotic

...reated wondrous flashes of light

... history. Love is a work of high

...ansaction of minds and bodies.

... undoubtedly needs the support

...anical, automatic processes pos-

...spirituality. The aspects of love

...le in aggregate are, when taken

...d, as I said, mechanical.

...for example, without sexual in-

...ke a brute force, like a brig uses

...n love" is another gross mecha-

...et off blindly, and love, good

...merely utilizes and harnesses it.

...he lofty life of the spirit, so esteemed in our culture, is impossible without the contribution of innumerable and inferior automatisms.

When we have fallen into that state of mental contraction, of psychic angina, of which falling in love consists, we are lost. During the first few days we can still fight; but when the disproportion between the attention paid to a woman and that which we devote to other women and the rest of the universe exceeds a certain measure, it is no longer in our hands to restrain the process.

Attention is the supreme instrument of personality; it is the apparatus which regulates our mental lives. When paralyzed, it does not leave us any freedom of movement. In order to save ourselves, we would have to reopen the field of our consciousness, and to achieve that it would be necessary to introduce other objects into its focus to rupture the beloved's exclusiveness. If in the paroxysm of falling in love we could suddenly see the beloved in the normal perspective of our attention, her magic power would be destroyed. In order, however, to gain this perspective we would have to focus our attention upon other things, that is, we would have to emerge from our own consciousness, which is totally absorbed by the object that we love.

We have been entrapped in an hermetic enclosure that has no opening to the outside world. Nothing from the outside is able to penetrate and facilitate our escape. The soul of a man in love smells of the closed-up room of a sick man—its confined atmosphere is filled with stale breath.

Falling in love automatically tends toward madness. Left to itself, it goes to utter extremes. This is well known by the "conquistadors" of both sexes. Once a woman's attention is fixed upon a man, it is very easy for him to dominate her thoughts completely. A simple game of blowing hot and cold, of solicitousness and disdain, of presence and absence is all that is required. The rhythm of that technique acts upon a woman's attention like a pneumatic machine and ends by emptying her of all the rest of the world. How well our people put it: "to suck one's senses"! [3] In fact: one *is* absorbed—absorbed by an object! Most "love affairs" are reduced to this mechanical play of the beloved upon the lover's attention.

The only thing that can save a lover is a violent shock from the outside, a treatment which is forced upon him. Many think that absence and long trips are a good cure for lovers. Observe that these are cures for one's attention. Distance from the beloved starves our attention toward him; it prevents anything further from rekindling the attention. Journeys, by physically obliging us to come out of ourselves and resolve hundreds of little problems, by uprooting us from our habitual setting and forcing hundreds of unexpected objects upon us, succeed in breaking

[3] *sorber los sesos* (Translator).

down the maniac's haven and opening channels in his sealed consciousness, through which fresh air and normal perspective enter.

At this point in our discussion it would be well to propose an objection which may have occurred to the reader while considering the previous chapter. When we define falling in love as a fixation of attention upon another person, we do not sufficiently draw a line between love and the thousands of situations in life in which serious and pressing political or economic affairs hold our attention to the utmost degree.

The difference, however, is radical. In falling in love, one's attention is voluntarily focused upon another person; whereas, in vital obligations, the fixation of attention is obligatory, against one's inclination. From a practical point of view, the most irritating thing about an annoying situation is being forced to attend to it. Wundt was the first—at least seventy years ago—to make the distinction between active and passive attention. Attention is passive when, for example, a shot is fired in the street. The unexpected noise imposes itself upon the spontaneous course of our consciousness and forces our attention. There is no such imposition upon the person who falls in love, for his attention is voluntarily given to the beloved.

A careful analysis of this phenomenon would reveal a curious two-sided situation in that we both willingly and unremittingly bestow our attention.

If understood in its finest implications, we can say

that whoever falls in love does so because he wants
to fall in love. This distinguishes falling in love,
which is finally a normal phenomenon, from obsession, which is a pathological one. The obsessed man
is not "fixed" upon his idea out of self-inclination.
What is horrible about his condition is precisely this:
that, though the idea is his, it presents itself to his
mind in the form of a tenacious external imposition,
which emanates from some anonymous, non-existent
"other one."

There is only one case, other than falling in love,
in which our attention is given voluntarily to another
person. It is the case of hate. Hate and love are, in
everything, hostile twins, identical and opposite. Just
as there is the act of falling in love, so there is—and
with no less frequency—an "act of falling in hate."

When we emerge from a period of falling in love
we feel an impression similar to awakening and
emerging from a narrow passage crammed with
dreams. Then we realize that normal perspective is
broader and airier, and we become aware of all the
hermeticism and rarefaction from which our impassioned minds suffered. For a time we experience the
moments of vacillation, weakness, and melancholy of
convalescence.

Once begun, the process of falling in love proceeds
with hopeless monotony. This is to say that all those
who fall in love fall in love the same way—the clever
man and the fool, the youth and the old man, the
bourgeois and the artist. This confirms its mechanical

nature. The only thing which is not purely mechanical about falling in love is its beginning. For that very reason we, as psychologists, are attracted by its beginning more than by any other phase of the phenomenon of love. What is it that draws the attention of a woman to a man and of a man to a woman? What qualities give one person the advantage over the indiscriminate array of others? There is no doubt that this is the most interesting subject of all; but, in turn, one of great complexity. Although all those who fall in love do so in the same way, not all fall in love for the same reason. There is no single quality which is universally loved.

Before entering, however, upon such a casuistic subject as what people love and of what the different types of erotic preference consist, it would be a good idea to point out the unexpected similarity which exists, in regard to paralysis of attention, between falling in love, mysticism, and, what is even more significant, the state of hypnosis.

7
Falling in Love, Ecstasy, and Hypnosis

The mistress of a house knows that her maid has fallen in love when she begins to notice that the maid is distracted. The poor servant's attention is not free for the things about her. She lives in a daze, drawn into herself, contemplating in her inner self the image of her ever-present lover. This concentration upon one's inner self gives the lover the appearance of a sleepwalker, a lunatic, someone "enchanted." Falling in love is, in fact, an enchantment; Tristan's magic potion has always symbolized with suggestive plasticity the psychological process of love.

In the expressions of everyday language, which condense millenary insights, there exist magnificent and yet untapped springs of extremely accurate psychology. It is always a certain "enchantment" which inspires love. Giving the name of a magical technique —enchantment—to the love object indicates to us that the anonymous mind, the creator of language, has observed the extraordinary and irresistible state into which the lover falls. The oldest form of verse, which was called *cantus* and *carmen*, is the magic formula. The ceremony and magical effect of the formula was the *incantatio;* hence *encanto* (in Spanish) or enchantment, and in French *charme* from *carmen*.

Regardless of love's relationship with magic, there exists, in my opinion, a more profound similarity between falling in love and mysticism than has heretofore been observed. We should have suspected this fundamental relationship in view of the remarkable coincidence with which the mystic employs erotic words and images to express himself. All those who have been interested in this religious phenomenon have observed the same thing, but they thought it could be adequately explained as an instance of metaphor.

The same thing happens with metaphors as with style. There are people who think that once they have classified something as a metaphor or a style the subject is closed and no further examination is needed— as if metaphor and style were not of equal stature with other realities, endowed with no less consistency and obeying laws and causes as forceful as those which govern sidereal rotations. If all those, however, who have studied mysticism have remarked upon the frequency of its erotic vocabulary, they have not observed the complementary fact which gives the former true gravity. This fact is that, vice versa, the lover tends to use religious expressions. For Plato, love is a "divine" madness, every lover calls his beloved divine, and feels "as if he were in heaven" in her presence, etc., etc. This curious interchange of vocabulary between love and mysticism leads us to suspect some common root.

The mystical process, as a psychological phenomenon, is in fact analogous to falling in love. It is so similar that it even coincides to the detail of being tiresomely monotonous. Just as falling in love occurs always in the same way, so mystics of every time and place have taken the same steps and have actually said the same things. Take any mystical book—Indian or Chinese, Alexandrian or Arabic, Teutonic or Spanish—and it will always deal with a transcendental guide, an itinerary of the mind toward God. The phases and vehicles are invariably the same, except for external and accidental differences.[4]

I understand perfectly, and *en passant* share, the lack of sympathy which the Church has always shown mystics, as if it feared that such ecstatic adventures might bring it loss of prestige. The ecstatic is more or less a madman. He lacks moderation and mental clarity. He gives an orgiastic quality to his relation with God which repulses the grave serenity of the true priest. The situation is such that, with extraordinary coincidence, the Confucian mandarin experiences the same contempt for the Taoist mystic as the Catholic theologian feels toward the visionary nun. Professional noisemakers of every class will always prefer the anarchy and intoxication of the mystics to the clear and ordered intelligence of the priests, that is, of the Church. I regret not being able to join them in this preference either. I am prevented by a matter of truthfulness. It is this: I think that any theology transmits to us much more of God, greater insights and ideas about divinity, than the combined ecstasies of all the mystics; because, instead of approaching the ecstatic skeptically, we must take the mystic at his word, accept what he brings us

[4] The only difference, and it is sometimes important, is this: some mystics have been great thinkers "besides," and along with the thread of their mysticism they communicate an ideology which, occasionally, is one of genius. Such was Plotinus or the Meister Eckhart. Their "mystique" as such is, however, identical to that of the most vulgar ecstatics.

from his transcendental immersions, and then see if what he offers us is worth while. The truth is that, after we accompany him on his sublime voyage, what he succeeds in communicating to us is a thing of little consequence. I think that the European soul is approaching a new experience of God and new inquiries into that most important of all realities. I doubt very much, however, if the enrichment of our ideas about divine matters will emerge from the mystics' subterranean roads rather than from the luminous paths of discursive thought. Theology—not ecstasy!

But let us return to our subject. Mysticism, too, is a phenomenon of attention. The first thing which the mystical technique proposes to us is to fix our attention upon something. Upon what? The most rigorous, studied, and famous ecstatic technique, Yoga, reveals most candidly the mechanical nature of all that will follow. Its answer to this question is: anything. It is not, then, the object which classifies and inspires the process; rather, it serves merely as a pretext for the mind to enter an abnormal state. One must, in fact, pay attention to one thing simply as a means of disregarding everything else in the world. We approach the mystical road by clearing our consciousness of the multitude of objects usually present and tolerated by the normal course of attention. In St. John of the Cross, for example, the point of departure for every ulterior advance is "the tranquil house." To stifle one's appetites and curiosity: "a great detachment from everything" or, as St. Theresa says, "an uprooting of the soul"—that is, cutting the roots and ligaments of our plural worldly interests, in order to be able to remain "absorbed" (St. Theresa) in one single thing. Identically the Hindu will stipulate this condition for entrance to mysticism: *nanatvam na pasyati*—turning away from multitudes and diversity.

This process of driving away things among which our attention is wont to wander is attained by sheer fixation of the mind. In India the exercise which makes use of any object was called *kasina*. For example: the contemplative makes a disc of clay, sits down next to it, and fixes his gaze upon it; or else from a height he watches a running brook, or contemplates a puddle in which the light is reflected; or else he starts a fire, places a screen before it, in which he makes a hole, and looks at the light coming through, etc., etc. Such contemplatives are seeking the same effect as the pneumatic to which I previously referred, which lovers employ to "absorb each other's senses."

There is never a mystical trance unless there is first a mental vacuum. "That is why," says St. John of the Cross, "God commanded the altar where sacrifices were to be made to be empty inside . . . so that the soul will realize how empty God wishes it to be of all other things." [5] A German mystic even more

---

[5] See Jean Bauzi's book: *Saint Jean de la Croix et le problème de l'expérience mystique*. Paris, 1924.

energetically expresses that withdrawal of attention from everything save one single thing—God—by saying: "I have been unborn." St. John himself says beautifully: "I do not watch over a flock"—that is, I have no preoccupation at all.

The most surprising thing, however, is that once the mind has been cleared of everything, the mystic assures us that he feels God before him, that he is filled with God; that is, God consists of precisely that vacuum. Consequently, Meister Eckhart speaks of the "silent desert of God," and St. John of the "dark night of the soul"; dark, but yet filled with light; so filled that, since there is sheer light, the light encounters nothing else and is darkness. This is the attribute of the spirit purged and annihilated of all personal preferences and interests, for by not liking or being interested in anything personal, that is, by dwelling in his vacuum, shadows and obscurity, he embraces everything with great ease, so that St. Peter's dictum: *Nihil habentes et omnia possidentes* (They have nothing and they possess everything) really applies to him. St. John elsewhere describes this complete vacuum, this luminous obscurity, with the most delightful formula: "It is," he says, "sonorous solitude."

We agree, then, that the mystic, like the lover, attains his abnormal state by "fixing" his attention upon an object, the function of which is, for the moment, simply to withdraw attention from everything else and permit a vacuum of the mind.

The most profound state of absorption, the summit of the path of ecstasy is not that in which the mystic disregards everything to gaze only upon God. The God whom it is possible to gaze upon is not truly God. The God who has limits and form, the God who is conceived in terms of this or that attribute, in sum, the God capable of being an object for one's attention, resembles, as such, things of this world too much to be the true God. Hence, the paradoxical feature of the doctrine, presented in the pages of mysticism time and again, which assures us that the supreme goal is not to think "even" of God. The reason for this is clear: through thinking about Him and being totally absorbed in Him, there comes a moment when He ceases to be something external to the mind and distinct from it, situated outside and in front of the individual. He ceases, in effect, to be *objectum* and becomes *injectum*.[6] God filters into the soul and merges with it or, inversely, the soul dilutes into God and no longer feels that He is a different being from itself. This is the *unio* (union) to which the mystic aspires. "The soul, that is, the spirit of this soul, remains as one with God," St. Theresa indicates in *La Morada Séptima*. Do not think that this union is felt as something momentary, first achieved and then

[6] See Otto: *Mysticism: East-West.* (Living Age Books, 1957).

lost. The ecstatic perceives it with the character of a definite, lasting union, as the lover who sincerely vows eternal love. St. Theresa emphatically distinguishes between both sorts of communication: one is "as if two wax candles were so close together that the light was all one. . . . But afterwards one candle can be easily separated from the other and they are again two candles." The other, however, is "as if water were falling from the sky into a river or fountain where it becomes all water and the water from the river and the water which fell from the sky can no longer be divided or separated, or as if a little stream empties into the sea and there is no way of separating them; or as if there were two windows in a room through which a great deal of light enters, and although it enters separately it all becomes one light."

Meister Eckhart has a very good argument for the relative inferiority of every state in which God is still an object of the mind. "True possession of God is in the spirit, not in thinking about God uniformly and continually. Man should not have a God who is merely thought about, for when his thought ceases, God would also cease." Therefore, the highest moment in the course of mysticism will be that moment in which the mystic feels saturated with God, like a sponge of divinity. Then he can again turn to the world and engage in earthly pursuits, because he is now actually working as an automaton of God. His desires, steps, and actions in the world will not be a thing of his own. Nothing that he does or that happens to him will matter any more, because "he" is removed from Earth, removed from his own desire or action, immune or impermeable to all sensitivity. His true self has migrated toward God, has been poured into God, and all that remains is a mechanical puppet, a "creature" which God controls. Mysticism, at its peak, always touches upon "quietism."

This extreme situation finds its equal in the development of "falling in love." When the other reciprocates, a period of transfusive "union" follows, in which each one transfers the roots of his being to the other and lives—thinks, desires, acts—not from himself but from the other. Here again the beloved is no longer an object to be thought about, for the simple reason that you have him within you. As with all inner states, this too is observable from the facial expression. In the period of "fixation," of absorbed, exclusive attention to the beloved who is still "outside," there is a corresponding look of engrossment and concentration. The eyes remain fixed, the gaze rigid, the head is prone to bow over the chest; the body, if it can, withdraws. The whole appearance tends to represent, in human form, something, as it were, concave and shut in. In the hermetic enclosure of our attention we are incubating the image of the beloved; but when the ecstasy of love arrives and the beloved is ours, that is, when the beloved has become myself and I have become the beloved, there appears upon the countenance a strange *épanouissement* in which happiness is expressed. One's gaze, softened by the eyes, becomes flaccid and passes over everything, observing little, of course, and, rather than seeing, seems instead to condescend to move lightly over various objects. Likewise, the mouth is always ajar, its drooping corners frozen in a perpetual smile. This is the expression of the fool—one of gaping wonder. Since there is no outer or inner object for us to behold, our soul loses its discipline and attitude of precision. We feel errant and ethereal, and all our activity is limited to allowing emanations from the surface of our being stream forth toward the absorbent sun, as from a still or quiet water ("quietism").

This is the common "state of grace" of the lover and the mystic.[7] They are not affected by this life and this world; for better or for worse, such things no longer matter to them. In our normal situation, things which we do and suffer affect our innermost being, become problems for us, cause us anxiety, and harass us. For that reason we feel our existence as a weight painfully supported by our own strength. But if we move that inner nucleus to another region or another person, outside the world, what happens then is that we lose our hold upon it and it remains suspended, as it were, in mid-air. As we pass through the real world we feel ourselves impregnable. It is as if there were two worlds with different but permeable dimen-

[7] As you see, I am not alluding at all to the religious "value" which pertains to the "state of grace." This is strictly the name of a psychological state inherent in all mystics of all religions.

sions. The mystic inhabits the earthly world in appearance only, for he really exists in the other, a region apart, which he and God alone inhabit. *"Deum et animam. Nihil ne plus? Nihil omnino,"* St. Augustine says. In the same way the lover moves among us, without our having any effect on him other than rubbing the surface of his sensibility. He has his life mapped out in advance and, he believes, forever.

In the "state of grace," whether mystical or sexual, life loses all weight and bitterness. With the generosity of a great lord the happy lover smiles upon everything about him. But the great lord's generosity is always in moderation and involves no effort. It is not a very expansive sort of generosity; actually, it originates in disdain. The man who thinks he is a superior being behaves "generously" toward people of an inferior class who can do him no harm, for the simple reason that he has no "dealings" with them and does not mingle with them. The height of disdain consists of not condescending to discover a fellow being's defects but, from our inaccessible height, projecting upon him the favorable light of our own well-being. Thus, for the mystic and the accepted lover, everything is lovely and charming. What happens is that on returning, after his period of absorption, to peruse things once again, he sees them not as they are but as they are reflected in the only thing which exists for him: God or the beloved. And what they lack in charm is liberally compensated for by the mirror in which they are viewed. According to Meister Eckhart: he who has renounced all things finds them again in God, like the man who turns his back on a landscape and finds it incorporeally reflected in the smooth and illusory surface of the lake. Or else the famous verses of our St. John of the Cross:

Overflowing with God's grace,
He passed through the groves in haste
And, though he saw them
In their natural state,
He left them garbed in beauty to his taste.[8]

The mystic, a sponge of God, is slightly overwhelmed by things until God, a liquid, seeps in and glosses them. So is the lover.

But it would be mistaken to thank the mystic or the lover for this "generosity." They applaud people simply because they view them without involvement. They pass and go on their own way. In fact, they are somewhat annoyed if they are detained too long, as is the great lord by the attention of "commoners." That is why St. John's expression is delightful when he says:

Move them aside, my beloved,
For I am in flight.

---

[8] *Mil gracias derramando,*
Pasó por estos sotos con presura,
Y yéndolos mirando
Con sola su figura
Vestidos los dejó de su hermosura.

The joy in the "state of grace," wherever it appears, depends upon being outside of the world and of oneself. This is, literally, what "ex-stasis" or "ecstasy" means: to be outside of oneself and the world. We ought now to mention that there are two irreducible kinds of men: those who experience happiness as a feeling of being outside of themselves, and those who, on the contrary, feel fulfilled only when self-possessed. From alcohol to mystical trances, the available means for getting outside of oneself are plentiful; similarly, there are many ways—from a shower to philosophy—to produce a state of self-possession. These two classes of men go different ways in every area of life. Therefore, there is the school of ecstatic art, for those to whom the enjoyment of art means "arousing their emotions." Others, on the other hand, claim that preservation of serenity is essential for true artistic enjoyment, since it enables a cool, clear contemplation of the object itself.

Baudelaire made a declaration of ecstasy when, in answer to the question of where he preferred to live, he said: "Anywhere, anywhere . . . provided that it is outside the world!"

The desire to "get out of oneself" has been the cause of all forms of orgiastic expression: drunkenness, mysticism, love. I do not mean to say by this that they all have equal "merit"; I am only insinuating that they belong to a common branch and that their roots are steeped in orgy. They are attempts to find respite from the weight of living separately by transferring ourselves to another being who will sustain and guide us. For this reason the simultaneous use, in mysticism and love, of the image of rapture or rape is not fortuitous. To be enraptured means not walking on one's own feet but feeling oneself carried by someone or something.

Rape was the primitive form of love, preserved in mythology in the guise of the centaur in pursuit of nymphs whom he bears away on his haunches. A vestige of this primitive abduction still remains in the ritual of the Latin marriage: the wife does not enter the new home on her own feet, but the husband lifts her in the air so that she does not step on the threshold. The ultimate symbolic sublimation of this phenomenon is the "trance" and buoyancy of the mystic nun and the lover's swoon.

This surprising parallel between ecstasy and "love" takes on, however, a more complex aspect when we compare both with another abnormal state of being: hypnotism. It has been noted hundreds of times that mysticism resembles hypnotism to a marked degree. In both there is a trance, hallucinations, and even identical physical effects, such as unconsciousness and catalepsy.

On the other hand, I have always suspected a strange connection between hypnotism and falling in love. I had been chary of formulating this idea, because the argument on its behalf was, in my opinion, that hypnotism seemed as well to be a phenomenon of attention. No one that I know of, however, has studied hypnosis from this point of view, notwithstanding the obvious fact that it depends, in its psychic aspect, upon the state of attention. Many years ago Claparède noted that we can induce sleep in proportion to our ability to stop thinking about things, to clear our attention of everything. The entire sleep-producing technique rests upon summoning our attention to focus upon some object or mechanical activity, for example, counting. You might say that normal sleep, like ecstasy, is self-hypnosis. But I notice that one of the most intelligent contemporary psychiatrists, Paul Schilder, believes that a close relationship between hypnotism and love must inevitably be recognized.[9] I shall try to summarize his ideas, since, being inspired by very different arguments than my own, they will conclude the cycle of coincidence which this essay has pointed out between falling in love, ecstasy, and hypnosis.

Here is the first series of coincidences between falling in love and hypnosis.

The devices which facilitate entrance into an hypnotic state have a sexual value: the soft, caress-like touches of the hand; the suggestive and, at the same time, tranquilizing talk; the "fascinating gaze"; sometimes a certain domineering violence of voice and gesture. When women are hypnotized, it frequently happens that, at the moment of falling asleep or im-

[9] *Ueber das Wesen der Hypnose*, Berlin, 1922.

mediately after awakening, the hypnotist is given that crushed look, which is so characteristic of sexual excitement or satisfaction. Often the hypnotized person declares that during the trance he experienced a delightful impression of warmth and well-being in his entire body. There is nothing strange about his recording decidedly sexual impressions. The sexual excitement is directed at the hypnotist, who upon occasion is publicly the object of amorous solicitation; and, sometimes, the sexual fantasies of a hypnotized woman are condensed into false memories and she accuses the hypnotist of having abused her.

Animal hypnotism supplies some related data. In the horrible species of spiders called *galeodes kaspicus turkestanus*, the female tries to devour the males who woo her. Only when the male succeeds in clutching with his claws a certain spot on the female's belly does she, in complete passiveness, permit the sexual act to be consummated. The act of paralyzing the female can be repeated in the laboratory, merely by touching that spot on the insect. She immediately falls into an hypnotic state. It is a noticeable fact, however, that such a result is obtained only during a period of heat.

After these observations, Schilder concludes: "All of this makes one suspect that human hypnosis is also an auxiliary biological modification of the sexual function"—and then he moves towards the everlasting Freudianism, whereupon he renounces all clear interpretation of the relations between hypnosis and "love." We can learn more from the notes in which he characterizes the psychic state of hypnotism. According to Schilder, it is a matter of relapse into a childish state of consciousness: the person delightedly feels that he has completely surrendered to another being and is resting under his authority. Without this relationship with the hypnotist, his influence would be impossible. Hence all that contributes to accentuate the hypnotist's elevated authority —fame, social position, a dignified appearance—facilitates his work. On the other hand, hypnosis cannot be accomplished in a human being if he does not wish it.

Note that all of these attributes can, unqualifiedly, be transferred to falling in love. The latter too—we have already observed—is always "wished for" and implicit in it is a desire to surrender oneself and to rest upon another being, a desire which in itself is delightful. As for the relapse into a mental state of relative childishness, it has the same significance as what I have called "contraction of the mind," a narrowing and impoverishment of the field of attention.

It is incomprehensible that Schilder does not even allude to the mechanism of attention as the most obvious factor in hypnosis, the hypnotic technique consisting principally, as it does, in the concentration of the attention upon one object: a mirror, a diamond point, a light, etc. Moreover, a comparison between different types of personality, in the order of their capacity to be hypnotized, shows a maximum coincidence with the scale which we would form of these same types in the order of their ability to fall in love. A woman is a better hypnotic subject than a man—*ceteris paribus*. But it is also true that she is more receptive to genuinely falling in love than is a man. Whatever the other causes may be which explain this tendency, it is without doubt immeasurably influenced by the different patterns of attention in the minds of the two sexes. Under equal conditions, the feminine psyche is closer to potential contraction than the masculine; for the simple reason that the woman has a more centripetal, integrated, and elastic mind. As we noted, the function charged with giving the mind its structure and cohesion is the attention. A highly unified mind presupposes a highly concentrated manner of attention. One could say that the feminine mind tends to have a single axis of attention, which at each phase of her life is set toward one thing alone. All that is necessary to hypnotize her or make her fall in love is to capture that single circuit of her attention. In contrast to the concentric structure of the feminine mind there are always epicenters in that of the man. The more masculine one is, in a spiritual sense, the more his mind is disjointed in separate compartments. One part of us is deeply dedicated to politics or business, while another devotes itself to intellectual curiosity and another to sexual pleasure. There is lacking, then, a tendency toward one unified gravitation of the attention. In fact, the contrary predominates, which leads to dissociation. The axis of attention is multiple. Accustomed as we are to existing upon this multiple base, with a plurality of mental fields which have a precarious connection among themselves, nothing happens when our attention is won over to one of them, since we remain free and intact in the others.

The woman in love usually despairs because she never seems to have the man she loves before her in his totality. She always finds him somewhat distracted, as if on the way to their meeting he had left sections of his mind scattered about the world. For this reason, the man always seems to be clumsy in love and incapable of reaching the perfection which the woman succeeds in giving to this sentiment.

In accordance with this, the same principle would explain the woman's propensity for mysticism, hypnosis, and love.

If we turn again to Schilder's study, we see that he adds a curious and important note of a somatic nature to the relationship between love and mysticism. Hypnotic sleep is not, finally, different from normal sleep; therefore the sleepy-headed individual makes an excellent hypnotic subject. A close relationship seems to exist between the function of sleeping and a place in the cerebral cortex called the third ventricle. Sleep disturbances, lethargic encephalitis, occur simultaneously with changes in this organ. Schilder thinks the somatic base of hypnotism is to be located here. But, at the same time, the third ventricle is an "organic node for sexuality," from which quite a number of sexual disturbances originate.

My faith in cerebral localizations is quite limited. It isn't hard to believe that if you chop off a man's head he will stop thinking and feeling. But this magnificent evidence begins to vanish progressively when we try to pin down and localize the nervous center of every psychic function. The reasons for this failure are innumerable; but the most obvious one consists of the fact that we do not know the true connection of the psychic functions and the order and hierarchy in which they work. It is easy for us to isolate a function descriptively and to speak of "seeing" or "hearing," "imagination," "memory," "thought," "attention," etc.; but it is unclear whether or not "thinking" overlaps with "seeing," or whether "attention" does or does not work in concert with "feeling." It is not easy to localize each function separately when the separations are not clear to us.

This skepticism, however, should stimulate an increasingly rigorous and advanced investigation. Thus, in the present case, the proper thing to do would be to test whether the faculty of attention has any direct or reflex effect upon that section of the cerebral cortex which, according to Schilder, is jointly responsible for sleep, hypnosis, and love. The close relationship which this essay intimated between these three states and ecstasy makes one suspect that the third ventricle also plays a part in mystic trances. This would ultimately explain the universal persistence of erotic vocabulary in ecstatic confessions and of mystical vocabulary in love scenes.

Recently, in his lecture in Madrid, the psychiatrist Allers refuted all attempts to consider mysticism as a derivative and sublimation of sexual love. I think his position is quite right. Early sexual theories of mysticism were generally quite trivial. But this is a different question. It is not a question of mysticism originating in "love," but of both possessing a common root and signifying two mental states with analogous organization. In each, the consciousness adopts an almost identical form, which elicits a similar emotive effect, and is equally manifested by mystical or erotic expression.

In closing this essay, I wish to remind the reader that I have tried exclusively to describe in it one single phase of the great amorous process: "falling in love." Love is a much broader and more profound operation, one which is more seriously human, but less violent. All love passes through the frantic zone of "falling in love"; but, on the other hand, "falling in love" is not always followed by genuine love. Let us not confuse, therefore, the part with the whole.

The quality of love is frequently measured by its violence. The preceding pages have been written to contradict this habitual error. Violence has nothing to do with love as such. It is an attribute of "falling in love," of an inferior, almost mechanical mental state, and can take place without love playing any real part in it.

There is in some cases a dearth of violence which proceeds, perhaps, from lack of sufficient energy in the lover. But, granted this exception, it must be said that the more violent a psychic act is, the lower it is in the hierarchy of the soul, the closer it is to blind physical mechanism, and the more removed from the mind. And, vice versa, as our sentiments become more tinged with spirituality, they lose violence and mechanical force. The sensation of hunger in the hungry man will always be more violent than the desire for justice in the just man.

the role of choice
in love

1

The essential core of our individuality is not fashioned from our opinions and experiences; it is not founded upon our temperament, but rather upon something more subtle, more ethereal and independent of these. We are, more than anything else, an innate system of preferences and distastes. Each of us bears within himself his own system, which to a greater or lesser degree is like that of the next fellow, and is always rigged and ready, like a battery of likes and dislikes, to set us in motion *pro* or *contra* something. The heart, an acceptance and rejection machine, is the foundation of our personality. Before knowing a total situation we find ourselves gravitating in one particular direction, toward certain particular values. Thanks to this, we are exceedingly wise about situations in which our preferred values are brought into play, and blind about others in which different, whether equal or superior, values exist which are alien to our sensibilities.

I wish to add to this idea, which is vigorously supported today by a whole group of philosophers, a second which I have not yet seen mentioned.

It is understandable that in living together with our fellow man nothing interests us so much as discovering what is his range of values, his system of preferences, for this constitutes the ultimate root of his being and the source of his character. Similarly, the historian who wishes to understand an epoch must, first of all, compile a list of the predominant values of the men of that time. Otherwise, the facts and statements which the documents of that age reveal to him will be a dead letter, an enigma and a charade, as are the words and acts of our fellow man if we have not penetrated beneath them and caught a glimpse of what values they serve in his secret self. This self, this nucleus of the heart, is, in fact, concealed to a great extent, even from ourselves who bear it within us—or, rather, who are borne by it. It acts in the subterranean penumbra, in the cellar of one's personality, and it is as difficult for us to perceive as it is to see the span of ground upon which our feet step. Neither can the pupil of an eye view itself. A good part of our lives, moreover, consists in the best-intentioned comedy which we ourselves play for our own benefit. We feign temperaments which are not our own, and we feign them in all sincerity, not to deceive others, but to enhance ourselves in our own eyes. Impersonators of ourselves, we speak and act under the motivation of superficial influences which the social environment or our will exercises upon our organism and which for the moment supplant our authentic lives. If the reader devotes a while to analyzing himself, he will discover with surprise —perhaps with fright—that a great part of "his" opinions and feelings are not his own, that they have not sprung spontaneously from his own personal self, but are instead stray ones, dropped from the social environment into his innermost valley, as dust from the road falls upon the traveler.

Acts and words are not, then, the best clues for identifying a neighbor's intimate secrets. Both are capable of being controlled and feigned. The thief who has made his fortune through crime can one fine day perform a philanthropic act, but he is still a thief. Instead of analyzing words and acts, it is better to notice what seems less important: gesture and facial expression. For the very reason that they are unpremeditated, they reveal information about profound secrets and generally reflect them with exactness.[1]

[1] The arguments which expound this revealing power which gestures, facial expression, handwriting and the way of dressing possess, appear in the essay "*Sobre la expresión, fenómeno cósmico,*" *El Espectador,* VII.

There are situations, moments in life, in which, unawares, the human being confesses great portions of
his ultimate personality, of his true nature. One of
these situations is love. In their choice of lovers both
the male and the female reveal their essential nature.
The type of human being which we prefer reveals the
contours of our heart. Love is an impulse which
springs from the most profound depths of our beings,
and upon reaching the visible surface of life carries
with it an alluvium of shells and seaweed from the
inner abyss. A skilled naturalist, by filing these ma-
terials, can reconstruct the oceanic depths from which
they have been uprooted.

Someone may wish to refute this with the presumed experience that frequently a woman whom we
consider to be of an eminent nature fixes her enthusiasm upon a stupid, vulgar man. But I suspect that
those who make this judgment almost always suffer
from an optical illusion: they speak from too great a
distance, and love, being a gossamer of such delicate
woof, can only be observed close up. In many instances, this enthusiasm is only apparent: in reality
it does not exist. Genuine and false love comport
themselves—when seen from afar—with similar movements. But let us imagine a case in which the enthusiasm is real: what ought we to think? One of two
things: either that the man is not so contemptible as
we think, or that the woman was not, really, of so
select a temperament as we imagined.

In conversations and in university courses (when

the occasion arises to define the meaning of what we call "character") I have repeatedly expounded this belief, and I have observed that it almost automatically provokes an initial reaction of protest and resistance. It is as if the idea itself contains some irritating or acid ingredient—why, as a general thesis, should we not flatter ourselves that our loves are a manifestation of our concealed beings?—and it is that automatic resistance which is tantamount to confirmation of its truth. The individual feels that he is caught by surprise, out in the open, because of a breach which he failed to close. We are always annoyed when someone judges us by some facet of our personality revealed by our negligence. They take us unawares, and this irritates us. We should like to be judged with forewarning and to pose, as for a photograph, with postures which we can control at will. (A terror of what is "instantaneous.") Of course, from the point of view of the investigator of the human heart, the most interesting adventure is to penetrate one's fellow man where he least expects it and to catch him *in flagranti*.

If man's will could completely supplant his spontaneity there would be no reason for delving into the recondite recesses of his personality. But the will can suspend the vigor of spontaneity only for a few moments at a time. In the course of a whole life, the intervention of will over character is practically nil. Our being tolerates a certain amount of falsification through the will: within this measure it is legitimate

to say that, rather than falsify, it completes and per-
fects us. It is the finishing stroke which the mind—
intelligence and will—gives to our primogenital clay.
Long may this divine intervention of spiritual power
remain in all its glory. It is necessary to modify one's
illusions about it, however, and not believe that this
marvelous influence can exceed a certain limit. Beyond this limit real falsification begins. The fact is
that a man who goes against his instinctive inclinations during his entire life is as a consequence in-
stinctively inclined to falseness. There are those who
are sincerely hypocritical or naturally affected.

The more present-day psychology penetrates the
mechanism of the human being, the more evident it
becomes that the role of the will and, in general, of
the mind, is not creative, but merely corrective. The
will does not incite, but rather deters this or that
involuntary impulse which animalistically rises from
the subconscious. Its intervention is, then, negative.
If it sometimes seems the contrary, it is for the following reason: it constantly occurs that, in the intri-
cacy of our inclinations, appetites, and desires, one
acts as a restraint upon the other. The will, when it
defers to this restraint, allows the previously shackled
inclination to flow and extend itself completely. It
seems that our "wanting" has an active power when,
actually, all that it has done is open the floodgates
that restrained an already existing impulse.

The greatest error, from the Renaissance to our
own day, lay in believing—with Descartes—that we

live out of our consciousness, that slight portion of our being that we see clearly and upon which our will operates. To say that man is rational and free is, I think, a statement very close to being false. We actually do possess reason and freedom; but both powers form only a tenuous film which envelops our being, the interior of which is neither rational nor free. The ideas, of which reason is composed, come to us readymade from a vast, obscure source located beneath our consciousness. Likewise, desires appear upon the stage of our clear minds like actors who appear from the shadowy, mysterious wings, in their costumes, reciting their lines. And just as it would be incorrect to confuse the theater with the play performed upon its illuminated stage, so I think it is at least inaccurate to claim that man lives out of his consciousness, out of his spirit. The fact is that, except for the superficial intervention of our will, we live an irrational life, which empties into our consciousness and which originates from our hidden source, the invisible depths which really define us. For the preceding reasons, the psychologist must be transformed into a diver and submerge himself beneath the words, acts, and thoughts of his fellow being, for they are but the surface that conceals the deeps. The things which are important lie behind the things that are apparent. For the spectator it is enough to see Hamlet dragging his neurasthenia through the fictitious garden. The psychologist, however, waits for him when he leaves the stage, and, in the penumbra of the curtain and the stage riggings, he wishes to know who the *actor* is that plays Hamlet.

It is natural, then, for him to look for trap doors and crevices through which he can slip into the hidden aspect of an individual. Love is one of these trap doors. It is in vain for the lady, who is trying to appear so exquisite, to attempt to deceive us. We have seen that she once loved so-and-so. So-and-so is stupid and coarse, and worries only about the perfection of his tie and the shine of his Rolls-Royce . . .

2

There are innumerable objections to the idea that we reveal our most authentic inner selves by our choice of lovers. Possibly there are among them some which are strong enough to destroy the truth of the assertion. However, I think those which one usually hears are inoperative, inexact, and improvised by hasty judgment. It is forgotten that the psychology of eroticism can only proceed microscopically.

The more inward the psychological theme with which one deals, the greater will be the influence of detail. The need for love is one of the most inward. Probably, there is only one other theme more inward than love: that which may be called "metaphysical sentiment," or the essential, ultimate, and basic impression which we have of the universe. This acts as a foundation and support for our other activities, whatever they may be. No one lives without it, although its degree of clarity varies from person to person. It encompasses our primary, decisive attitude toward all of reality, the pleasure which the world and life hold for us. Our other feelings, thoughts, and desires are activated by this primary attitude and are sustained and colored by it. Of necessity, the complexion of our love affairs is one of the most telling symptoms of this primogenital sensation. By observing our neighbor in love we are able to deduce his vision or goal in life. And this is the most interesting thing to ascertain: not anecdotes about his existence, but the card upon which he stakes his life. We all realize to some extent that the kind of life to which we are committed is already determined in areas deeper than those in which our will is active. Turning experiences and arguments over and over in our minds is futile: our hearts, with the obstinacy of a star, are committed to a predetermined orbit, which will revolve by its own gravitation toward art, political ambition, sexual pleasure, or money. Many times, the surface existence of an individual rubs against the grain of his inner destiny, and surprising disguises are the result of this friction: the businessman who conceals a sensualist, or the writer whose only real ambition is political power.

The normal man "likes" almost every woman he encounters. This fact permits the nature of profound choice, which love possesses, to stand out all the nore. It is necessary, however, that one not confuse liking and loving. The good-looking girl who passes by produces an excitation in the periphery of masculine sensibility, which is much more impressionable—let it be said to his credit—than that of a woman. This excitation automatically produces his first move in her direction. So automatic and mechanical is this reaction that not even the Church dares to consider it as a form of sin. In former times the Church was an excellent psychologist. It is a pity that it has fallen behind during the last two centuries. The fact is that the Church clairvoyantly recognized the innocence of "first moves." Thus it is that the male feels attracted and lured on by the woman who clicks along on high heels in front of him. Without these preliminaries there would be none of the rest—neither the good nor the bad, neither the virtue nor the vice. The expression "first move" does not say, however, all that it should. It is "first," because it emerges from the periphery where it has received the stimulus, without the person's inner self having participated in it.

The attraction which almost every woman exerts upon a man and which amounts to a sort of instinctual call to the profound core of our personality is, in fact, usually not followed by any response, or only by a negative response. The response would be positive if a feeling of involvement with what has just attracted our periphery burst forth from our utterly personal core. Such a feeling, when it arises, joins the core or axis of our souls to that external sensation;

or, said in another way: we are not only attracted at our periphery, but, by ourselves, go toward that attraction, and put our whole being at its disposal. In sum: we are not only attracted, but we show interest. One is as different from the other as being dragged is different from moving voluntarily.

This interest is love. It acts upon the innumerable attractions which are experienced, eliminating most of them and focusing only upon one. Therefore, it produces selection in the extremely broad area of instinct, whose role is thereby recognized and at the same time limited. Nothing is more needed, in order to clarify the better the workings of love, than to define with some exactness the role which sexual instinct plays in them. If it is an absurdity to say that a man's or woman's true love for one another has nothing sexual about it, it is another absurdity to believe that love can be equated with sexuality. Among many characteristics which make the two different, is this fundamental one: instinct tends to amplify indefinitely the number of objects which satisfy it, whereas love tends toward exclusivism. These contrasting tendencies are clearly manifested in the fact that nothing immunizes a male against other sexual attractions so well as amorous enthusiasm for a *certain* woman.

Love, then, in its very essence, is choice. And since it springs from the personal core—the spiritual depths—the selective principles which determine it are at the same time the most intimate and mysterious preferences which form our individual character.

I have indicated that love, living on details, proceeds microscopically. Instinct, on the other hand, is macroscopic and is active in the presence of the whole. One could say that both operate from two different distances. The kind of beauty which attracts one is seldom the kind of beauty which makes one fall in love. If the indifferent man and the lover could compare what beauty means to each of them or what constitutes the charm of one and the same woman, they would be amazed at the incongruity. The indifferent man will find beauty in the broad lines of her face and figure—what, in fact, is usually called beauty. For the lover these sweeping lines—the architecture of the beloved person as seen from afar— do not exist; they have disappeared. If he is sincere, he will find beauty in separate little unrelated aspects: the color of her eyes, the way her mouth turns, the sound of her voice, etc.

When he analyzes his feeling and follows its course from within himself to his beloved, he notes that the thread of love is inextricably bound up with these little aspects, and constantly receives sustenance from them. There is no doubt that love is continually being fed; it derives nourishment from the beloved's charms, which it beholds either in reality or in imagination. It lives in the realm of ceaseless confirmation. (Love is monotonous, incessant, boring; no one would stand for anyone's repeating the most ingenious statement so many times and, yet, the lover demands unending reiteration that his beloved loves him. And vice versa: when someone is not in love, love bestowed upon him oppresses him and drives him mad by its utter plodding quality.)

It is important to emphasize the role which facial details and gesture play in love, because they are the most expressive means of revealing a person's true character, and hence are instrumental in our choice. That kind of beauty which, when viewed from a distance, reveals not only a personal character and a mode of being, but also an independent esthetic value—an objective plastic charm—is what we allude to by the noun *beauty*. It would be a mistake, I think, to believe that it is this plastic beauty which incites a man's ardor. I have always noticed that men seldom fall in love with the most plastically beautiful women. There are a few "official beauties" in every society, whom people point to with their fingers in theaters and at parties, as if they were public monuments; however, personal masculine ardor is rarely directed toward them. Such beauty is so decidedly esthetic that it converts the woman into an artistic object, and, by isolating her, places her at a distance. She is admired—a sentiment which implies distance—but she is not loved. The desire for intimacy, which acts as love's advance guard, is rendered impossible by mere admiration.

The expressive charm of a certain manner of being, and not correctness or plastic perfection, is, in my opinion, the quality which effectively inspires love. And vice versa: when an individual finds himself involved in a false instead of true love—whether for reasons of self-love, curiosity, or pigheadedness—the mute incompatibility which he feels with certain aspects of the other person is the first indication that he is not in love. On the other hand, a lack of correctness or perfection of appearance, from the point of view of pure beauty, is not an obstacle to love if it is not of grotesque proportions.

The idea of beauty, like a slab of magnificent marble, has crushed all possible refinement and vitality from the psychology of love. People think that in saying that a man has fallen in love with a woman whom he thinks good-looking they have said everything. This error has its origin in the Platonic inheritance. (No one can estimate the penetration of concepts of ancient philosophy into the ranks of western civilization. The most uneducated man uses words and concepts from Plato, Aristotle, and the Stoics.) It was Plato who made the everlasting connection between love and beauty; although by beauty he did not mean precisely physical perfection. Beauty was, rather, the name for all perfection, the form, to put it another way, in which anything worthy appeared to the Greeks. Beauty was superiority. This peculiarity in vocabulary has led subsequent thinking on eroticism astray.

Loving is something more serious and significant than being excited by the lines of a face and the color of a cheek; it is a decision on a certain type of human being, symbolically presented in the details of the face, voice and gestures.

"Love is a desire for generation and birth in beauty (*tiktein en tô kalô*)," Plato said. Generation is creation of a future. Beauty is the good life. Love implies an inner adherence to a certain type of humanity which to us seems the best and which we find preconceived, inherent in another being.

And this, my dear madame, probably sounds abstract, abstruse, and removed from concrete reality. Nevertheless, guided by this abstraction, I have just discovered in the look you gave to X what life means to you. Let's have another cocktail!

3

In most cases a man is in love several times during his lifetime. This fact raises a number of theoretical problems, in addition to the practical ones which the lover will have to solve on his own. For example: is this successive continuum of love affairs part of masculine nature, or is it a defect, a licentious remnant of primitivism and barbarism which still survives? Would a single love be the ideal, perfect and desirable thing? Is there any difference, in this matter, between the normal woman and the normal man?

For the moment we are going to avoid every attempt to answer such dangerous questions. Without allowing ourselves to take a stand on them, we accept, without much ado, the indisputable fact that the male is almost always pluralistic in love. Since we are discussing, however, the pure forms of this sentiment, the simultaneous existence of several love affairs is excluded and we are left with those which occur successively.

Does the fact of male pluralism present a serious objection to our thesis that choice in love reveals the essential nature of a person? Perhaps; but first it is worthwhile to remind the reader of the trivial observation that this diversity of love affairs can be of two classes. There are individuals who in the course of their lives love several women; but with clear persistency each one is a repetition of a single feminine type. Sometimes, the coincidence is so great that these women even share the same physical features. This kind of masked fidelity, in which actually a single generic woman is loved under the guise of many women, is exceedingly frequent and constitutes the most direct proof of the idea which we hold.

But in other cases, the women successively loved by a man, or the men preferred by a woman, are, in truth, very different types. If this fact is considered from the point of view of our previous idea, it would mean that the man's essential nature had changed from one time to another. Is such a change in the very roots of our being possible? The problem is of a crucial, and perhaps decisive, nature in any study of character. During the second half of the nineteenth century it was customary to think that the direction of character formation moved from the outside inwards. The experience of life, the habits they engender, the influences of the environment, the vicissitudes of fortune, physiological conditions, would, like a well, decant that essence which we call character. There would not be, then, an essential nature of an individual, there would not be any inner structure prior to and independent of the happenings of existence. We would be formed, like a snowball, from the dust on the road which we travel. According to this way of thinking, which obviates any radical nucleus in the personality, there does not exist, of course, the problem of radical changes. So-called character would be constantly modified: in the same way as it is being made it is also being unmade.

Arguments of sufficient weight, which this is not the time to enumerate, make me lean to the opposite belief: it seems more exact to say that we live from the inside outwards. The essential lines of our inner character are already formed prior to the occurrence of external contingencies, and although the events of one's existence do have some influence upon character, the influence which character exercises upon events is much greater. We are incredibly impervious to what befalls us when it is not in harmony with that innate "character" which, in the final analysis, we are. "In that case," you will say, "there is no point in even talking about fundamental character changes. What we were when we were born we will be at the hour of our death."

Indeed not. This opinion possesses enough flexibility to be adaptable to situations of every variety. It allows us to distinguish between the slight modifications which external events introduce into our mode of being and other deeper changes which are not founded on those grounds of chance, but on the very nature of character itself. I would say that character does change, if change is properly understood to be an evolution. And this evolution, like that of any organism, is induced and guided by internal reasons, inherent in the person himself and as innate as his character. The reader has most probably had betimes the impression that his neighbor's transformations are frivolous and unjustified, that they are foreign to his innermost self, but that in other instances the change possesses complete dignity and every visible sign of growth. It is like the seedling which becomes a tree; it is the naked tree before the leaves; it is the fruit which follows the foliage.

This is my answer to the former objection. There are people who do not develop, who, relatively speaking, are mentally stagnant (in general, those with little vitality: the prototype, the "good bourgeois"). They will persist in an invariable scheme of amorous choice. There are, however, individuals of a fertile nature, rich in possibilities and destinies, who patiently await their moment of blossoming. You can almost say that this is the normal case. A personality experiences in the course of its life two or three great transformations, which are like different stages of the same moral trajectory. Without losing solidarity, or even the fundamental homogeneity of yesterday's feelings, we notice one day that we have entered upon a new phase or modulation of our characters. Such modulation we call a fundamental change. It is nothing more, and nothing less.[2] Our innermost being seems, in each one of these two or three phases, to rotate a few degrees upon its axis, to shift toward another quadrant of the universe and to orient itself toward new constellations.

Is it not a meaningful coincidence that the number of true loves which the normal man usually experiences is almost always the same in number: two or three? And, moreover, that each of these loves appears chronologically localized in each of these stages in character? Therefore, I do not think it extravagant to see in the plurality of loves the sharpest confirmation of the doctrine I am suggesting. A new mode of reacting to life results in a vigorous change, and it is but a normal consequence that a different type of woman should be preferred. Our system of values has been altered to a greater or lesser degree—always in potential harmony with the old one; qualities which we previously did not value and of which we may not

[2] The most curious and extreme phenomenon is "conversion," the sudden tumultuous change which a person sometimes undergoes. Allow me to leave this difficult subject untouched for now.

even have been aware, emerge into the foreground, and a new pattern of erotic selection is interposed between the man and passing woman.

Only the novel offers an adequate vehicle to illustrate this idea. I have read selections from one—which perhaps will never be published—whose theme is precisely this: the profound evolution of a masculine character seen through his loves. The author—and this is what is interesting—also insists on showing the continuity of the character in the course of his changes and the divergent contours which these changes possess, thus elucidating, with living logic, their inevitable genesis. At each step the rays of that evolving vitality are gathered and concentrated in the figure of one woman, like the images formed by light in a dense atmosphere.

Parenthesis

My essays, which usually appear in sections, like the sections of an annelid, in the newspaper El Sol,[3] provide me with an agreeable pretext for getting to know the minds of Spanish men and women outside my personal orbit, of whom I would otherwise be unaware. I receive, in fact, with flattering frequency, letters of corroboration, protest, or disagreement. My activities prevent me from answering these epistolary gestures, which are so useful and fruitful for an au-

[3] Ortega was the founder and editor-in-chief of El Sol, a Madrid newspaper which still appears. (Translator)

thor, although answering them would be both correct and at the same time delightful. In the future I shall occasionally try to skim from this correspondence what seems most fertile and of most general interest.

To begin with, I shall reproduce an anonymous letter which comes to me from Cordova. The man who wrote it seems to be very intelligent, except for the fact that he remains anonymous.

I have read your series in El Sol, "The Role of Choice in Love," just as I read everything of yours that falls into my hands in order to enjoy your subtle and original observations. This favorable predisposition toward your work encourages me to point out something which I consider incorrect in your latest article.

Agreed that gesture and facial expression allow us to penetrate another's surface and make ourselves at home, due to the careless (and perhaps also the vigilant) attitude of our neighbor. So much do I agree with you on this point, that I have written and published something on it.

In my opinion, the thing that cannot really be upheld is that "by the choice of his lover the male reveals his essential nature; by the choice of her lover, the woman hers," and that the type we prefer outlines the contours of our heart.

I would even dare to affirm that those automatic protests which such a statement generally elicits in your listeners are, rather than a disturbing uneasiness of finding themselves unexpectedly naked before an observer, the result of opposition, perhaps unreasoned opposition, to an idea we do not accept, an idea that we cannot accept, although we do not yet know why.

Love (sexual passion, with or without the lyrical furbelows), a noun derived from an eminently transitive verb, is in a sense the most intransitive, the most hermetic of all verbs, because it begins and ends in the individual, it is nourished by his very being, and the only life it possesses is that which this very individual himself gives to it.

To be sure, the lover, out of sexual hunger, seeks out an individual of the opposite sex, and each wishes to find certain desirable physical dimensions in the other; but it would not be at all strange for an eminent representative of womanhood to focus her ardor upon a vulgar man, and vice versa.

The lover can indeed be known by his love; but not by the object of his love. Each person loves with the fullness of his spirit, and with sufficient force to project into his beloved all the niceties and refinements that the lover's soul (that is to say, his own soul) requires, like the magic lantern or motion picture casts its lines and color on the screen, or like Don Quixote projected into Aldonza Lorenze and Nelson into Lady Hamilton (the deer in the landscape in the early nineteenth century)[4] the elements

---

[4] See the essays "Landscape with a Deer in the Background" and "Love in Stendhal" in this collection. (Translator)

needed to make their souls fall prostrate before these two women.

And now I shall close, because this, in synthesis, is my objection and I do not wish to trouble you unnecessarily.

I am most thankful for the objection, except that I would prefer receiving more forceful ones. The attempt to reduce love to sexuality at once clouds the issue *a limine*. In the series of articles, "Love in Stendhal," which *El Sol* published this fall, I believe I demonstrated the obvious error in this simplification. All one has to do is observe the inalterable fact that a man, with varying degrees of intensity, feels sexual desire for innumerable women, whereas his love, no matter how excessive and prolific it may be, is only focused upon a few. It becomes impossible, therefore, to equate the two impulses. But, furthermore, my kind correspondent says that "each person loves with the fullness of his spirit." In such a case, love could hardly be mere "sexual hunger" and nothing more. And if it is more, if spirit adds its heterogeneous collaboration to the mating instinct, we will end with a psychic activity which is very different from mere instinct. It is this activity which we call love.

It is not correct, moreover, to classify such a substantial addition as "lyrical furbelows." One moment of calm near the well, among the geraniums, while passing clouds glide over the Cordovan patio, would be ample time in which to establish the different meanings of the words "love" and "desire." This clever Cordovan would then see that love and desire or appetite are not at all alike, although one may be elicited by the other. One may sometimes grow to love what he desires: we desire what we love, *because* we love it.

There was a time—for example, that of the "resentful" Remy de Gourmont—in which it seemed analytically superficial to permit oneself to be "deceived" by the rhetoric of love, and the sexual drive was thereby stressed (*Physique de l'amour*). Truly, the role of this instinct in man has been highly exaggerated. When this pejorative and perverse psychology was started—at the end of the eighteenth century —Beaumarchais promptly said that "drinking without being thirsty and loving at any time is the only thing which differentiates man from animal." All well and good; but what must be added to the animal who is a "lover" once a year to make of him a "creature" who "loves" all four seasons of the year? Even if we remain on the lowest level of sexuality, how is it possible for man, who is remarkably painstaking about love, to spring from the animal who is so indolent in this matter? We soon come to the realization that sexual instinct, strictly speaking, practically does not exist in man, but is almost always found to be indissolubly united, at least, with fantasy.

If man did not possess such an excellent, fertile imagination, he would not "love" sexually, as he does,

upon every possible occasion. Most of the consequences imputed to instinct do not spring from it. If
they did, they would also appear in the animal. Nine-
tenths of that which is attributed to sexuality is the
work of our magnificent ability to imagine, which is
no longer an instinct, but exactly the opposite: a creation. I merely wish to observe that the notorious disproportion between the sexuality of man and woman,
which makes the normally spontaneous woman so
conservative in "love," probably coincides with the
fact that the human female usually enjoys less imaginative power than the male. Nature, cautiously
and foresightedly, wanted it that way, because if the
opposite had occurred and the woman were endowed
with as much fantasy as the man, licentiousness
would have flooded the planet and the human species
would have disappeared, volatilized in sensuousness.[5]

Since this idea, which does not see any reality in
love other than sexual instinct,[6] is very widespread
and deeply imbedded in people's minds, I thought it
worthwhile to publish the letter from Cordova,
which gives us one more pretext for undertaking the
elimination of this view.

[5] Lust is not an instinct, but a specifically human creation—
like literature. In both, the most important factor is imagination. Why don't psychiatrists study lust from this angle—as
a literary genre which has its origins, laws, evolution and
limits?

[6] If, besides physical instinct, the soul also has instincts, as I
believe, the discussion should rest on a very different basis.

The anonymous letter ends by recognizing that "the lover can be known by his love; but not by the object of his love." To this I would answer, avoiding extraneous verbiage: first, how is it possible to become acquainted with the love of a lover by the direct method, if, as are all sentiments, it is part of a hidden inner realm? The choice of the object is the only gesture which permits us to divine it. And, secondly, if the lover gives his all to love, is it by chance that he chooses one woman and not another? Why is it that this highly intelligent reader does not avoid relapsing into that other view, which, next to the sexual interpretation, is responsible for closing most roads in the psychology of love—Stendhal's "crystallization"? According to this idea, the charms which we fancy to be in the beloved would always be imaginary. Being in love would be in fact but an example of being mistaken. I have been openly attacking this idea, which enjoys much better fortune than it deserves. My arguments against it can be summed up in two points. First, it is unlikely that any normal activity of man is based upon an essential error. Love sometimes errs, as the eyes and ears may err. But, like these, its abnormality is based upon general accuracy. Second, imaginary or not, love is excited by certain real charms and qualities. It always has an object. Although the real person may not coincide with this imaginary object, some grounds of affinity must exist between the two which leads us to fancy one woman, and not another, as the foundation and subject of those charms.

4

The idea that there is choice in love—a choice which is more real than many which are made consciously and deliberately—and that this choice is not free but, rather, depends upon the individual's basic character, must at once seem unacceptable to those who hold the psychological interpretation of man which has, in my opinion, failed and ought to be substituted.

The psychological interpretation of man is based on the tendency to exaggerate the intervention of chance and the mechanical contingencies of human life. Sixty or more years ago men of science carefully tested this point of view and sought to construct a mechanistic psychology. As always happens, their ideas have taken a generation to penetrate the consciousness of the average educated man. Unfortunately, at the present time, every new attempt to see things more exactly encounters minds filled with outmoded ideas. Aside, then, from the fact that the thesis here suggested may be true or false, it must of necessity clash with general currents of thought which are of a conflicting tendency. People have become accustomed to thinking that events, the totality of which forms their existence, do not have any meaning, either good or bad, but rather that they come about through a combination of chance and mechanical fate. Every idea that reduces the role of these two elements in the destiny of the person and tries to discover within the person some inner law based on the individual's character, will immediately be rejected. A swarm of false observations—in this case, on the "love affairs" of our fellow beings or on our own—quickly chokes the opening through which a new view could penetrate the mind, be understood and judged. Add to these difficulties the habitual misinterpretations which almost always consist of spontaneous additions with which the reader embellishes the author's idea. Most of the objections which I receive belong to this category. The most frequent among these consists of the observation that if we molded the woman, whose being is assumed to reflect our own, the unhappiness which follows passion or even accompanies it would not occur so often. This attitude suggests that these particular readers have arbitrarily connected the affinity between the lover and his beloved, which I upheld, with consequent unhappiness. One has nothing to do with the other. A man who is vain to the core—as "bluebloods" generally are, no matter how decadent they may be—will fall in love with a woman who is also vain. The consequence of this choice is, inevitably, unhappiness. Let us not confuse the consequences of the choice with the choice itself. At the same time, I wish to answer another class of very elementary and very obvious objections which, being elementary and obvious, are constantly reiterated. It is said that, in many cases, the lover errs in judgment, imagining his chosen beloved to be one type of person and subsequently discovering her to be another. Is this not one of the most repeated plaints in the usual psychology of love? If one were to believe this, erroneous judgments would almost be considered the *quid pro quo* of normal situations. Here our roads part. I cannot accept, without a great many convincing arguments, any theory by which human life, in one of its most profound and most serious activities—such as love—turns out to be a sheer and almost consistent absurdity, oddity, and mistake.

I do not deny that mistakes can occasionally result, as happens in physical vision, but these do not invalidate the accuracy of our normal perception. If, however, error is insistently presented as the normal occurrence, I must say that I think this view is inaccurate and that it results from insufficient observation. Error, in most of its presumed examples, does not exist: the person is what he at once appeared to be, except that later we suffer the consequences of his particular mode of being. It is this that we call our mistake. For example: it is not uncommon for a young bourgeois girl of Madrid to fall in love with a man for a certain looseness and audacity that his person exudes. He is always above circumstances, ready to resolve them with an admirable coolness and authority which are definitely the result of an absolute disregard of everything divine and human. One cannot deny that such flexibility in movement, at first glance, gives this type of male a charm which is usually lacking in more profound personalities. He is, in short, of that species known as the *calavera*[7] or the playboy. The girl usually falls in love with the *calavera* before he performs his escapades. Shortly afterward, he pawns her jewelry and abandons her. Friends of the little lady unsuccessfully console her for her "mistake"; but deep within her being she knows very well that it was no unanticipated "mistake," for she had suspected such an outcome from the beginning, and her suspicion was one element of her love, the thing in him that "appealed" to her most.

I think that we must begin reforming the topical ideas of this magnificent sentiment, because love is now in a very confused state, especially on our Peninsula. A splendid triggering of human vitality—which, after all, not many enjoy—love should be clearly defined and freed from sordid attachments. Let us be cautious, then, in supporting the idea of "error" when we are trying to explain the recurring drama of eroticism. I deplore the fact that the intelligent anonymous writer from Cordova, in another letter, resorts to the idea that we fall in love with the

---

[7] I do not know where this amusing expression of our language comes from, and if any reader should conclusively know its origin I would be very grateful if he would communicate it to me. I suspect that it has to do with the scenes of cemetery rape which the "golden youth" made stylish during the Renaissance.

"physical proportions" of the beloved, and since similar physical types "harbor very different and even contrary psyches," errors occur. Such errors, he believes, make it impossible to affirm an affinity between the object that is loved and the nature of the lover. The fact is that, in his first letter, this courteous native of Averroes recognized that a person's inner self shows through in his gestures and facial expression. I regret that I cannot accept the separation (which is another of the great manias of the past epoch) between what is physical and what is psychical. It is false, and completely false, that we see "only" a body when we see, in fact, a human figure before us. It would be as if by another and later mental act we could magically add to this material object, by unknown means, a psyche taken from nobody knows where! [8] On the contrary, the actual fact is that it is very difficult for us, supposing that it can be done at all, to separate and abstract the body from the soul. Not only when living with another human being but even in a casual relationship, the visual image we have of a person's body is simultaneous with our psychical perception of his soul or quasi-soul. In a dog's howl we perceive his pain, and in a tiger's eye his ferociousness. Only by this means can we distinguish a stone and

[8] See my essay *"La percepción del prójimo,"* in the volume *Teoría de Andalucía* (2nd ed.) p. 81, and especially Scheler's great work, *Wesen und Formen der Sympathie,* 1923.

machine from body and flesh. Flesh is essentially
a physical body charged with psychic electricity;
in short, with character. The fact that at times
equivocal forms exist and we err in the perception of another's soul will not serve, I repeat, to invalidate normal accuracy.[9] When we are confronted
with another creature of our species his inner state is
at once revealed to us. This penetration of our fellow
man exists to a greater or lesser degree, depending
upon our intuitive perception. Without it the most
elementary dealings and social relationships would
be impossible. Every word and gesture which we
would make would offend our interlocutor. And just
as we are made conscious of the gift of hearing when
we speak to a deaf man, so are we made conscious of
the normal intuition which men possess in their dealings with one another when we encounter an indiscreet person, a man without "tact" [10]—an admirable expression this, which alludes to that sense of
spiritual perception with which one seems to touch
someone else's soul, to feel its contours, the harshness
or gentleness of its character, etc. Most people cannot "say" what the person before them is like, but
being unable to "say" does not imply that one is

[9] On this great matter of the expressive value of the body
I again refer the curious reader's attention to my essay
"*Sobre la expresión fenómeno cósmico*" (*El Espectador*, VII).

[10] In Spanish "*tacto*" has a double significance: "tact" and
"sense of touch." (Translator's Note)

unable to see. "To say" is to express oneself in concepts, and the concept presupposes a specifically intellectual and analytic activity which few individuals have mastered. Knowledge which is verbally expressed is superior to that which is satisfied with having something before its eyes; but the latter, too, is a kind of knowledge. Let the reader try to describe in words what he is seeing at any moment, and he will be surprised at how little he can "say" about what he so clearly sees in front of him. Nevertheless, this visual knowledge is useful as a guide for our movements in the world of objects; it aids us in differentiating them—for example, the nameless shades of a color—and in seeking or avoiding them. The insight we have into our fellow man, especially in the case of love, acts upon us in the same extremely subtle way.

Do not repeat, then, so calmly, as if you were saying something clear and simple, that a man falls in love with a woman "physically," and that shock at her character follows subsequently. What actually happens is that some people of both sexes fall in love with a body as such; but such action precisely reveals their specific mode of being. It is the lover possessed of a sensual character who suggests this preference; but it is necessary to add that such lovers are far less frequently encountered than people think. In women this condition is especially rare. For this reason, whoever has observed the feminine soul with care will doubt whether a woman's erotic ardor for masculine beauty is a normal occurrence—and usually he can predict what types of women will be the exception to this rule. They are: first, women with a slightly masculine nature; second, those who undoubtedly have practiced unlimited sexual freedom (prostitutes); third, normal women who have behind them a fully practiced sexual life and are now reaching maturity; fourth, those who through their psychological make-up are endowed with "great temperament."

These four types of women possess a common quality which defines their marked weakness in the presence of male beauty. As is well known, the feminine soul is much more integrated than that of the male; that is, the elements of a woman's nature cohere more thoroughly. As a consequence, the disassociation of sexual pleasure and love or ardor is less frequent in her than in the man. In the woman, the one is not aroused without the other. If this is so, there must be a very special reason to cause feminine sensuality to become independent and to act according to its own particular law. In the four types of women mentioned earlier, the germ of this disassociation may be found. In the first, the degree of masculinity which she possesses results in less integration and a more sharply defined separation of her various faculties. (Masculinity in woman is one of the most interesting subjects of human psychology and deserves a separate study.) In the second, the disassociation is produced by the profession itself, so that the prostitute, more than anyone else, is sensitive to the handsome man (presuming, of course, that the prostitute is not an exceptionally peculiar case of masculinity in a woman). In the third, which is perfectly normal, I refer to the fact that, as is commonly said, "a woman's senses are slow to be aroused." The truth is that they are slow in freeing themselves, and only the woman who, even though observing all conventions, has had a prolonged and energetic sexual life, really achieves full release of her sensuality. In the man, excess of imagination can substitute for actual practice in effecting sensual development. In the woman —when she is not masculine—the imagination is generally impoverished and this defect may be largely attributed to the habitual modesty of the female.

5

If love is so decisively a matter of choice as I assume it to be, we shall possess in it simultaneously the *ratio cognoscendi* and the *ratio essendi* of the individual. As in Esquilys' simile, corks floating on the sea foam are a sign of the net scraping along the uneven bottom, so love will serve us as a criterion and a sign for understanding the lover's moral subsoil. On the other hand, it contingently acts upon the person's life by introducing into its innermost part a particular type of individual and eliminating the rest. Love in this way models individual destiny. I believe we do not take into sufficient consideration the enormous influence which our loves exercise upon our lives; this, because we primarily think only about the most superficial, although seemingly dramatic aspects of love—the "follies" that a man commits for a woman, or vice versa. Since, however, the greatest part of our lives, if not the whole, is free from such follies, we tend to underestimate the extent of love's influence. The fact is that this influence generally acquires a very subtle aspect, especially in the case of a woman's effect upon a man's existence. Love unites individuals in such close and all-embracing relation, that it leaves no room between them to perceive the reform which one is producing upon the other. The woman's influence is, especially, atmospheric and, for that reason, ubiquitous and invisible. There is no way of preventing and avoiding it. It creeps in through the gaps in one's caution and subtly acts upon the man in love as climate does upon a plant. Its individual attitudes toward life bear down gently and continually upon the characteristics of our soul and end by transmitting to the soul its own peculiar distortion.

This leads us to the disclosure of several important insights into the idea that love is a profound desire. If, instead of restricting ourselves to the single individual, we extend the doctrine to all the individuals of a period—for example, a generation—we will notice the following: whenever one speaks about the multitudes and masses, the extremes of individual uniqueness are offset and an average type of behavior stands out; in this case, an average type of amorous preference. This is only to say that each generation prefers a general type of male and another general type of female, or, what amounts to the same thing, a certain group of types in both sexes. Since, finally, matrimony is numerically the most important form of erotic relationship, we can say that in every period a preponderance of one type of woman will marry rather than another.[11]

As does the individual, each generation reveals in the choice of its loves the undercurrents which give it form. This is true to such an extent that one of the most instructive avenues for assessing human evolution would be to attempt a history of the feminine types which have successively been preferred. Moreover, as does each generation, each race distills a prototype of femininity which is not produced spontaneously, but modeled in one long secular labor, by virtue of the majority of men coinciding in their preference for it. Thus, a careful, dispassionate outline of the nature of the archetypal Spanish woman would cast astounding light upon the secret recesses of the peninsular soul. To make her portrait stand out clearly she would have, of course, to be compared with the archetypal French woman, the archetypal

[11] I do not believe it necessary, for the purpose of this particular application, to recall the well-known rules governing every law or valuation based upon a great mass of cases, rules upon which statistics bases its accuracy. In a very considerable number of cases, instances of a most diverse sort are to be found; but one predominates, and the exceptions cancel each other out. In any period women of all types get married; but one predominates and is qualitatively and quantitatively favored.

Slavic woman, etc. The most fruitful aspect of this investigation, as of all such inquiries, lies in perceiving that things and peoples are what they are not merely because of sheer and spontaneous generation. No! Everything that is, everything in the world that has form, whatever it may be, is a product of some force, a vestige of some energy and a symptom of some activity. In this sense, *everything has been made*, and it is always possible to inquire into the power that has forged each thing and in so doing, left its everlasting mark upon it. The acts of the entire history of Spain are preserved in the moral portrait of the Spanish woman, like the hammer blows struck in fashioning a chalice.

The important thing, however, about the amorous preference of a generation is its causal power; because not only does its own existence depend upon the type of woman that it chooses but, in good part as well, the existence of any subsequent era. In the home the dominating climate is always that which the woman is and introduces. No matter how much the man "commands," his role in family life is disconnected, peripheral and official. The home is essentially the every-day occurrence, the continuous activity, the indefinite series of identical minutes, the habitual air which the lungs tenaciously inhale and respire. This domestic atmosphere emanates from the mother and immediately envelops the generation of her children. The latter may be of the most diverse temperaments and characters; but inevitably they have been developing under the pressure of that atmosphere, a common level to which they have been destined, an unceasing wind which has imposed a peculiar curvature upon them. The slightest difference in life attitudes on the part of today's preferred woman, multiplied by the constancy of its influence and the large number of homes where it recurs, results in an enormous historical modification when seen over thirty years. In no way do I claim that this is the only important factor in history; but indeed it is one of the most active. Imagine the consequence if the general type of female preferred by boys of today is slightly, only slightly, more dynamic than the one loved by our parents' generation. The children will, of course, be propelled toward a slightly more audacious and enterprising existence, more marked by appetites and experiments. No matter how small the change in vital tendency, it will, extended over the average life of the nation, inescapably produce a gigantic transformation of Spain.

Note that the decisive factor in the history of a nation is the average man. The tenor of the national strength depends upon him. By this, I do not wish to deny the existence of eminent individuals, elevated figures, who exert a powerful role in the destinies of a race. Far from it! Without them there would be nothing worthwhile. But, regardless of their elevation and perfection, they will affect history only to the extent that their example and influence impregnate the average man. What can we do about it? History is, irremissibly, the rule of the mediocre. The only capital quality Humanity possesses is the "H" with which we adorn it typographically. The greatest genius is shattered against the unlimited force of vulgarity. The planet, apparently, is made for the average man to continually rule. The important thing, therefore, is for the median level to be elevated as high as possible. What makes a nation great is not primarily its great men, but the stature of its innumerable mediocre ones. Of course, in my opinion, the average level will never be elevated without the existence of superior examples, models who challenge the inertia of the multitudes and attract them toward lofty heights. That is why the role of the great men is only secondary and indirect. It is not they who are the historical reality, for it is possible for a nation to possess individual geniuses without the nation's being worth the more for it. This always happens when the masses are indifferent to their examples, when they do not follow them and do not perfect themselves.

It is curious that historians, until recently, occupied themselves exclusively with extraordinary facts and freak events and were unaware that these possess merely an anecdotal or, at most, partial value. Historical reality is rather to be located in the everyday occurrence, the immense ocean in whose vast dimensions everything unexpected and outstanding is drowned.

Wherever the everyday occurrence governs, the

woman, whose soul is formed to a great extent by daily events, is always a factor of major importance. The man always leans more toward the extraordinary, at least he dreams of adventure and change, with tense, difficult, and unique situations. The woman, on the other hand, feels a truly strange fulfillment in the details of everyday life. She is comfortable amid inveterate habits and, to the best of her ability, she will make a yesterday out of today. I have always believed the idea of *souvent femme varie* to be a lot of nonsense, an opinion hastily formed by a man in love with a woman who plays with him a while. But the wooer's point of view has a very limited horizon. When the woman is studied from a greater distance and with a calmer eye, with a zoologist's gaze, it is seen with surprise that she tends to the utmost to take her time in whatever engages her, to take root in the custom, idea, or task set before her; in sum, to make a habit out of everything. And the persistent lack of understanding which in this respect exists between the two sexes is consequently touching: the man goes to the woman as to a party or an orgy, to an ecstasy which will break the monotony of his existence, and almost always he finds a person who is only happy when engaged in everyday tasks, whether it be darning underwear or going dancing. So true is this that, with great surprise certainly, ethnographers show us that work was invented by women; work, that is, as the compulsory everyday chore, in contrast to enterprise, and such spontaneous activity as sports and adventure. For this reason it is the woman who creates trades: she is the first agriculturist, collector and ceramicist. (It has always seemed strange to me that, in an essay by Gregorio Marañón entitled *Sex and Work,* this very elementary and evident fact is not taken into account.)

When one reads between the lines of daily life the dominant force of history, one begins to understand the gigantic feminine influence on ethnic destinies, and becomes especially concerned with the type of woman who has stood out in our nation's past and the type that is beginning to be preferred in our time. I understand, however, that this preoccupation is not frequent among us, because, upon speaking of the Spanish woman, everything is resolved merely by recalling the presumed inheritance from the Arabs and the role of the priest. Let us not discuss now the measure of truth inherent in such a thesis. My objection to it is foregone and is based upon the following observation: presuming these two formative agents of the Spanish feminine type to be real, women would then appear to be solely the product of male influence, and, therefore, this thesis does not even suggest the reciprocal influence of the woman upon herself and upon our national history.

6

What was the type of woman in Spain preferred by the generation prior to ours? Which type do we love? Which will the new generation presumably choose? This is a subtle, delicate and compromising subject, as subjects one writes about ought to be. (Why write, if this too easy activity of pushing a pen across paper is not given a certain bull-fighting risk and we do not approach dangerous, agile, and two-horned topics?) In this case not only is an extremely important matter being treated, but it is incomprehensible that it, and equally important ones, are not dealt with more frequently. A financial law or a rule of distribution is discussed at length, but, on the other hand, the sentimental tendencies which carry in their arms, as it were, the entire life of our contemporaries, is neither commented upon nor analyzed. And, nevertheless, political institutions depend in no small measure upon the predominant type of woman. Whoever does not find a close correlation between the Spanish Parliament of 1910, for example, and the type of wives which the politicians had at that time in their homes, is blind. I should like to write about all this, even with the foreknowledge that I would probably be wrong in nine-tenths of my ideas; but this sacrifice of making a mistake in good faith is almost the only public virtue which the writer, as such, can offer his fellow man. The rest are the empty gestures of a soapbox orator or a café bench-warmer, cheap heroics which do not spring from the special organ of his profession: intelligence. (For ten years, many Spanish writers have sought in politics a pretext for not being intelligent.) But before attempting to sketch the predominant feminine portrait of the present Spanish era—I am planning a separate study for this—I wish to carry this idea of choice in love to its ultimate far-reaching conclusion.

In passing from the single individual to the masses of a generation, amorous choice is converted into selection, and our own idea merges with Darwin's great theory—sexual selection, a gigantic force which contributes to the forging of new biological forms. It is noteworthy that this magnificent scheme has not been fruitfully applicable to human history: it remained restricted to the corral, the sheepfold, and the jungle. It lacked one wheel to function as an historic idea. Human history is an inner drama: it takes place within souls. It was necessary, therefore, to transpose sexual selection to that inner stage. Now we shall see that in man this selection is made by choice, and this choice is ruled by profound ideals, fermented in the innermost depths of the person.

Darwin's idea lacked this wheel and, moreover, possessed a superfluous one: in sexual selection the best adapted and preferred types were the ones that were selected. This theory of adaptation is the superfluous wheel. As is known, it deals with a vague, imprecise idea. When is an organism especially well adapted? Isn't everyone well adapted except sick people? On the other hand, can't you say that nobody is completely so . . . etc., etc.? It is not that I abhor the principle of adaptation, without which it is impossible to get anywhere in biology, but rather that it is necessary to give it much more complex and sinuous forms than those which Darwin gave it and, above all, to commit it to a secondary position. It is false to describe life as adaptation. Without a minimum of adaptation it is impossible to live; but the surprising thing about life is that it creates audacious, extremely bold and primarily unadaptable forms, which, notwithstanding, manage to adjust themselves to minimal conditions and succeed in surviving.

Every living species can and should be studied from two opposite sides: as an outstanding phenomenon of maladaptability and whim and as an ingenious mechanism of adaptation. One would say that life plants a seemingly insoluble problem in every species in order to give itself the pleasure of resolving it, generally in a grand and elegant manner. This is true to such an extent that in studying living forms one scans the breadth of the cosmos, seeking for the understanding onlooker, in the hope of whose applause merry Nature has taken all these pains. We are completely unaware of the ultimate ends which govern sexual selection in the human species. We can only uncover partial results and ask ourselves a few delightfully indiscreet questions. For example, this one: Has there ever been a period when it was normal for a woman to prefer the best type of existing man? Scarcely is the question posed, when we discern the grave duality: the best man for a man and the best man for a woman are not the same. I strongly suspect that they have never been the same.

Let us say it, in all crudity, that women have never been interested in geniuses, unless it were *per accidens;* that is to say, when in addition to the genius of a man there were overshadowing qualities which were scarcely compatible with his genius. One thing is certain: the qualities which are generally most esteemed in a male, for the good of progress and human greatness, do not at all interest the woman erotically. Do you mean to tell me that it does not matter to a woman if a man is a great mathematician, a great physicist, or a great politician, etc., etc.? It is true that all specifically masculine talents and efforts, which have engendered and broadened culture and excite masculine ardor, have no bearing in themselves on the attracting of a woman. On the other hand, if we look for the qualities which enamor her, we find that they are the ones least fruitful for the general perfection of the species and those which least interest men. The genius is not "an interesting man" according to the woman, and, vice versa, the "interesting man" does not interest men.

An extreme example of a great man's ineffectuality in his encounters with women is Napoleon. We know his life minute by minute and we have a complete account of his overtures to women. Napoleon was not lacking in physical appeal. As a young man, his sharp slenderness gave him the graceful air of a fine Corsican fox; later he rounded out imperially, and his head became exceptionally handsome from the masculine point of view. The fact is that even his physical proportions have inspired the fervor and fantasy of artists—painters, sculptors, poets. Women could well have become enraptured with him. But not at all: with a great likelihood of telling the truth, it can be affirmed that no woman ever fell in love with Napoleon, the master of the world. They all felt restless, out of sorts, and ill at ease near him; they all thought what Josephine had the sincerity to say. While the young impassioned general dropped jewels, millions, works of art, provinces, and crowns into her lap, Josephine, deceiving him with the first dancer who came along, received his treasures and exclaimed, in surprise: *"Il est drôle, ce Bonaparte,"* gliding over the *r* and stressing the *l,* as French créoles usually do.[12]

It is distressing to observe the dearth of feminine warmth amid which the poor great men have usually lived. One would say that genius horrifies a woman. The exceptions strengthen the full impact of this observation: self-evident though it is, it becomes even more striking if a multiplication process, demanded by reality, is carried out upon it. I am referring to the following:

In the process of love it is necessary to make a distinction between two states, the confusion of which

---

[12] The relations between Napoleon and Josephine are well described in Octavio Aubry's book, *Le roman de Napoléon: Napoléon et Josephine,* 1927.

clouds the psychology of eroticism from beginning to end. In order for a woman to fall in love with a man, or vice versa, it is necessary for her first *to take notice* of him. This taking notice is nothing other than a concentration of attention upon a person, thanks to which the latter stands out and is elevated above the common plane. Such favor in attention knows nothing yet of love but is a preliminary condition to it. Without the first taking notice, the amorous phenomenon cannot take place, although the latter need not necessarily follow. Of course fastening one's attention upon something creates such a favorable atmosphere for the germination of ardor, that it alone is normally equivalent to a beginning of love. But it is of extreme importance to differentiate between the two moments, because different principles govern in each. A good number of errors in the psychology of love originate in the confusion between the qualities which "attract one's attention" and, thereby, make an individual stand out favorably, with those qualities which are truly endearing. Wealth, for example, is not what is loved in a man; but a wealthy man stands out before a woman because of his wealth. A man famous for his talents possesses, in short, a superior chance of being noticed by a woman. This is sufficiently so that if the woman does not fall in love it is difficult to find an excuse. Such is the case of the great man, who generally enjoys dazzling notoriety. The indifference which the feminine sex feels toward him should, therefore, be multiplied by this important factor. The woman, consciously and not by accident, disdains the great man.

From the point of view of human selection, this fact means that the woman in her sentimental preferences does not collaborate, in the same way as does a man, in the perfection of the species. She tends rather to eliminate the best individuals, speaking from a masculine viewpoint—those who innovate and undertake lofty enterprises—and she manifests a decided enthusiasm for mediocrity. When one has spent a good part of his life with an alert eye, observing the comings and goings of women, it is not easy to harbor any illusion about the standard of her preferences. All the good intentions, which she sometimes shows, of becoming excited about superior men usually fail dismally and, on the other hand, she is seen swimming to her taste, as if in her element, when she circulates among mediocre men.

This is the conclusion prompted by observation, but do not believe that in formulating it there is any implicit censure of the woman's normal nature. I repeat that Nature's ends remain an ultimate mystery. Who knows if finally this indifference of women toward what is best is not for the good? Perhaps her role in the mechanics of History is to be a retrogressive force in the face of the turbulent restlessness and the desire for change and advance which springs from the masculine soul. The fact is that, taking the matter in its broadest horizon, and as it were zoologically, the general tendency of feminine zeal seems resolved to keep the species within mediocre limits, to avoid selection in the sense of choosing what is superior, to endeavor never to allow the man to become a semi-god or archangel.

IV

thoughts on standing before the Marquesa de Santillana's portrait

In my opinion, the most interesting portrait in the Exhibition[1] is that by Jorge Inglés. If the feminine schemes suggested in it had been fulfilled, this collection of four centuries of feminine portraits would be very different, and so would have been the history of Spain.

This picture is so feminine that it is at first deceptive. In the hurried passer-by it leaves the memory of a tranquil, secluded enclosure, filled with the peace of prayer. Upon the *prie-dieu*, which serves as

---

[1] This refers to a *Retrospective Exhibition of Spanish Feminine Portraits* which the Sociedad de Amigos de Arte presented in 1918.

a little mystical ship, a woman's spirit sets sail toward celestial abstractions.

There is nothing more feminine, I repeat, than to present two very different aspects: one for the person who passes by, another for the one who attentively stops. If one wishes to know a woman, it is necessary to stop in front of her, or, said in another way, it is necessary "to flirt." There is no other method of becoming acquainted. Flirting is to a woman what experimentation is to electricity. The flirtation begins with detainment, thanks to which the passer-by is transformed into an interrogator initiating a particular conversation. When Ferdinand LaSalle, the precursor of the present labor movement, was going to marry, he gave the news to a friend, parodying Hegelian terminology by writing: "I am going to individualize myself in a woman." Actually, a woman does not reveal her second aspect, her true, personal aspect, except to the man who individualizes himself before her, who ceases being merely a man in general, a passer-by, an "anyone." In this, as in everything, the woman's psychology is the opposite of the male's. The masculine soul, by contrast to the woman's, preferably projects its life toward collective works: science, art, politics, business. This provides us men with somewhat theatrical dispositions: we give the best, most personal and individual side of ourselves to the public, to the nameless numbers who read our writings, applaud our verses, vote for us in elections, or buy our merchandise. The writer represents the extreme form of this immodesty, for he is more intimate with the anonymous public than with his most intimate friend. Man lives because of others, and therefore he lives for others. This is what I was alluding to when I spoke about the servility attached to the masculine destiny.

The woman, on the other hand, has a more regal attitude toward existence. She does not allow her happiness to depend upon the benevolence of the public, nor does she submit what is most important in her life to its acceptance or rejection. On the contrary, she adopts, in fact, a public attitude, by which *she* appears to be the one who approves or disapproves of the approaching man, the one who selects and chooses him from among many others. The effect of this is that the man, upon seeing that he is the one who is preferred, feels rewarded. It is curious that this conception of the woman, as man's prize, appears in the most ancient societies. The *Iliad*, for example, unfolds its sonorous multitude of hexameters in order to recount the anger of Achilles, who was infuriated because the gentle slave Briseis, a prize for his deeds, was snatched away from him. Subsequently, the value of this prize increases until it is not granted by the authorities or by a tribunal, but is left to the prize herself to decide who the prize-winner shall be.

Compared with man, every woman is something of a princess: she lives from herself and, therefore, she lives for herself. She presents to the public only a conventional impersonal mask, although variously modulated; she follows the fashion in everything, and takes pleasure in clichés and accepted ideas. Her fondness for finery, jewelry, and make-up might be considered to constitute a radical objection to what I say. In my opinion, far from contradicting it, this confirms it. A woman's vanity is more ostentatious than a man's, precisely because it concerns itself only with externals: it is born, lives, and dies in that external surface of her life to which I have referred; but it does not generally affect her inner reality. The proof of this is that the vanity in ostentation, common in a woman, does not allow us to infer characteristics of her nature with the same certainty as in a man. Male vanity, although less ostentatious, is more profound. If talent or political authority were to show on one's face, as does beauty, the presence of most men would be intolerable. Fortunately, these superiorities do not consist of stationary traits, but of actions and dynamisms which require time and effort to be executed; which cannot be shown, but must be demonstrated.

So marked is the difference between a man's and a woman's relationship with the public that it produces opposite signs. The more preparations and attentions the woman affects when appearing in public, the greater the distance she establishes between her public and her true personality. In like proportion as the adoration with which a woman surrounds herself increases, the number of males who feel eliminated from the right to her preferences increases and they know that they are doomed to the role of distant spectators. One could say that the purpose of the luxury and elegance, adornment and jewelry which a lady places between herself and others is to conceal her inner self, to make it more mysterious, remote, and inaccessible. The man, on the other hand, publicizes what he most esteems in himself, his most profound pride, those acts and labors into which he has poured the seriousness of his life. The woman possesses a theatrical exterior and a circumspect interior, while in the man it is the interior that is theatrical. The woman goes to the theater; the man carries it inside himself and is the impresario of his own life.

I do not find this radical discrepancy sufficiently emphasized in the usual ideas on the psychology of the sexes. It is a question of two opposite instincts: in the man there is an instinct of expansion and self-revelation. He feels that if what he is does not appear in plain view of others, it is as worthless as if it did not exist. It is for this reason that he desires confession and the exposure of his inner self. Lyricism definitely originates in this genial male cynicism. Sometimes, this proclivity toward self-expression (as if in transmitting the self to others it acquired its full-blown reality) degenerates into mere contentment with saying things, however non-existent their basis. The inner lives of a good number of men do not extend beyond words, and their sentiments are limited to an oral existence. There is in the woman, on the contrary, an instinct of concealment and secrecy: her soul lives as if its back were toward the outside world, hiding its inner passionate fermentation. Gestures of modesty are merely the symbolic form (see Darwin and Piderit) of this inner reserve. It is not actually her body, but rather her reactions to the man's intentions toward her body, which she wishes to defend from his glances. Confusion in a woman most frequently and most intensely arises from the same origin. This emotion is aroused by the fear of being caught off guard in her thoughts and inclinations. The greater our desire to keep something about our inner lives secret, the more exposed we are to confusion. It is usual, for example, for someone telling a lie to become confused, as if he were afraid that another's gaze would see through his mendaciousness and expose its true concealed meaning. The woman lives, however, in perpetual confusion, because she lives in perpetual self-concealment. A girl of fifteen generally has a greater number of secrets than an old man, and a woman of thirty more arcana than a Chief of State.

This possession of a personal, separate, and secret life, this lordship of an inner sanctum in which no one else is permitted to roam, is one of woman's superiorities over man. This is what constitutes a woman's innate "distinction," the tenuous, mystical means for placing a distance between herself and us. This "distinction" is, as Nietzsche saw very well, above all a *"pathos* of distance" between one individual and another. In view of woman's "distinction."

friendship between women may be less intimate than between men. One could say that they possess a very clear awareness of where their own incommunicable life begins and where the next person's ends.

The real feminine existence, therefore, flows along masked and concealed, protected from the public by an apparent femininity constructed for the purpose of serving as a mask and plate of armor. I think that every intensely personal life has always had to isolate a fictitious personality, a kind of *dermato-psyche* to hold off and distract the hostile curiosity of inferior people, in order to be able, behind that bulwark, to devote itself freely to being what it is. This mask-personality—the exception in men—turns out to be natural in women.

A man usually forgets this essentially latent quality. In his dealings with women, he goes, therefore, from one surprise to another. Normally, the first impression of a woman excludes the possibility that that delicate, playful, ethereal figure, all disdain and subterfuge, is capable of passion. Every woman appears to be a little saint, if we think that saintliness consists in sliding over life without letting oneself be compromised by it. And, yet, the truth is exactly the opposite: that almost unreal figure is merely awaiting the opportunity to throw herself—with such impetus, decisiveness, courage, and unconcern for painful consequences—into an impassioned whirl-wind, that she outdoes the most resolute man, who sheepishly discovers himself to be of a practical, calculating, and vacillating temperament. In order, however, for that profound, individual vitality of the woman to assert itself for him, the man must cease being a part of the anonymous public, and for some reason or other must stand out as an individual in her eyes. The thing that is repugnant and monstrous about the prostitute is her contradiction of feminine nature, by virtue of which she offers the anonymous man, the public, that hidden personality which ought to be revealed only to the chosen one. To such a degree is this a negation of feminine character, that a scrupulous man feels an instinctive aversion toward the prostitute, as if, in spite of her female body, there were a masculine spirit in her. On the other hand, the "classic" example in feminine matters, Don Juan, is preferably attracted by the most modest woman, the one who hides herself most completely from the public, who, in feminine morphology, represents the opposite pole from the prostitute. Don Juan, in fact, falls in love with the nun.

From spectator and public the man passes, by means of the *flirtation,* to an individual relationship with the woman. Starting a *flirtation* is an invitation to a *tête-à-tête,* a furtive spiritual communication. It begins, therefore, with a gesture, a word which disregards and as it were removes the conventional mask, the woman's surface personality, and knocks at the door of that more intimate personality. Then, like the moon which emerges from among the clouds, the concealed woman begins to radiate her hidden vitality and relinquish her fictitious countenance before the man. This moment of spiritual denudification, that brief period in which the superficial, impersonal woman is transformed into the real, individual woman (a phenomenon which can be compared to the exposure of a photographic plate) produces in the man the greatest spiritual delight. Don Juan's vice is not, as a plebeian psychologist assumes, brutish sensuality. On the contrary, historical figures who, by their traits, have contributed to the ideal character of Don Juan, were distinguished by an abnormal frigidity toward sexual pleasures. Don Juan's crime is in compelling woman after woman to "open up" in that miraculous scene, that pathetic instant in which the larva, in honor of a man, turns into a butterfly. When the scene is ended, the cold grimace returns to Don Juan's lips, and, leaving the butterfly to burn her newly spread wings in the sun, he turns toward another chrysalis.

The instance of this portrait, in which Jorge Inglés perpetuates the Marquesa de Santillana's image, provides a pretext for this and innumerable considerations. At first glance we find a lady preoccupied in prayer, cherubically submerged in a quiet, abstract, and liturgical atmosphere. If we persist, we shall see the external impassioned butterfly emerging from the picture, eagerly flying toward the light.

As I have said, this picture contains a delightful duality. At first it seems to us to be filled with tranquility and a vague odor of incense; however, if we persevere, we notice in it the germination of all sorts of restlessness, and through the grillwork on the window and the oratory door we feel a terrestrial breeze enter which blows (with gentle turbulence) the lady's fine hair.

The technique displayed in the picture is irresolute: two pictorial principles fight their indecisive battle in the hand of the artist. The North and the South, Flanders and Italy, pursue each other in every corner of the canvas, like Hector and Diomedes in a Homeric chant. This pictorial vacillation is only a symptom of a grave contest which implicates the entire work, from the master's inspiration up to the very nature of the person portrayed: here in hand-to-hand combat are Gothicism, which is of the Middle Ages and of asceticism, and the Renaissance, which is a sign of a new era and a triumph of this world over the other.

The lady has been perpetuated in the act which the Middle Ages preferred: prayer. Nevertheless, let us look carefully. The hands aspire toward the empyrean. What is holding them back? Why are they fluttering about in the air like the wings of a lost dove? Nobody knows exactly why, nobody. There is an essential ambiguity in human gestures, and when someone raises the palms of his hands together, we do not know whether it is to bury himself in prayer or to throw himself into the sea. The same gesture prefaces two opposite adventures.

The Marquesa de Santillana, therefore, is setting her hands on the *prie-dieu,* but she has not forgotten to encircle every phalanx of every finger with a festive ring. They are delicate rings, set with a ruby, a garnet, an amethyst, and a sapphire. The ceremonial dress of this marchioness ripples forth magnificent perfumes of the courts of love.

Her husband, an amiable poet, personifying the most vigorous outbursts of the Renaissance in Spain, had gleaned the heritage of Provençal lyricism, the same as had Dante and Petrarch. Perhaps that is why the lady's silhouette brings to our mind those Provençal palaces where, in the eighteenth century, under the name of *cortezía,* the cult of loftier human instincts made its surreptitious entrance into theological society.[2]

[2] The Modern Age, of which we are so proud, is the offspring —in its science, politics, and arts—of the Renaissance. The Renaissance is, in turn, the offspring of Provençal culture which flourished in the thirteenth century. This Provençal culture rose under the protection of a few genial women who invented the *ley de cortezía,* the first break with the ascetic, ecclesiastic spirit of the Middle Ages. Nothing indicates more the incapacity of our period to understand history than our forgetting this fundamental fact. Let it be clear, then, that it is neither the engineers nor the professors who have initiated progress in their laboratories and their universities, but a few flowery ladies and the parties in their salons, then called "courts." The recent scientific bibliography in which this is proved and, in general, the ideological development of the subject, can be seen in an essay on which I am working: *De la cortesía o las buenas maneras.*

The subtle drama of the protrait has been so concentrated in the gentle head, endowed with such strange expressive vigor, that it succeeds in triumphing over the complicated hairdo and the artist's inadequacy. With what grace that little face, to which an inferior hand has added a pair of apocryphal eyes, vibrates in the breeze, like a flower in the meadow! The features lack ordinary beauty which is satisfied with perfection: they are fine distinguished features, whose worth lies in the spirit they reveal.

The expression of some women's faces sums up an attitude toward life and can serve as a standard for guiding our behavior and controlling our judgments. When Goethe, surfeited with germanic inelegance, went down to Italy in search of a more refined vital order, he was engaged in the composition of *Iphegenia*. When passing through Boulogne he stopped before Raphael's *Santa Agata*. "The artist," he wrote in his diary, "has given her a wholesome, self-assured maidenhood, free from coldness and severity. I have studied the face a great deal, and I shall find in it the spirit of my Iphegenia, because nothing should come out of the lips of my heroine which this Saint might not be able to say." Since a literary work for Goethe was not a thing apart from his own personal life, these words mean that the great dissatisfied German, upon passing before Raphael's painting, changed the shape of his thinking to adapt it to the pattern radiated by that face.

One cannot ask this much from Jorge Inglés' painting. But there are germs of a possible superior existence in it, which, if developed, could define the lives of those of us who live on this slope of the Guadarrama, where the Marquesa de Santillana once dwelt. A breath of exquisite vitality passes through this little figure, making it quiver, but nowhere else in the rest of the Exhibition does this phenomenon again appear. When we reach Goya's canvases we shall again find vitality in his women, but no longer will we find exquisiteness.[3]

Far be it from my intention to place in doubt the piety with which this lady is praying, but if I try to clarify for myself the position of her head and of her hands, I inevitably imagine the movement which the deer makes when, from the depths of the shade, she hears in the distance the sound of the first "halali!" which resounds through the limits of the woods. Without knowing where it comes from, an impassioned excitement has struck the heart of this marchioness. We suspect that she is in the oratory on her way to some passion. Now you can hear it, you can hear the gallop of perfect gentlemen, and the instinctive frantic barking of the dogs. The lady feels a mysterious desire to flee. Nothing else is needed for the eternal hunting scene to unfold. In the hunt, the

[3] Such an opinion seems extravagant, since such portraits as *La Duquesa de Alba* and *la Tirana* are in the exhibition. Nevertheless, I refer the reader to what I shall, in its place, say about these two admirable figures.

mission of the quarry is to flee, dragging the hunter and the pack of hounds in its whirlwind of pursuit. So, in the frenzy of love affairs, the woman at first collaborates with an appearance of terror and of flight . . .

Let others think what they like: for me, the culmination of life consists of a pure and subtly dramatic passion.

V

landscape with a
deer in the background

(Albert Flament: *La vie amoureuse de lady Hamilton,* 1927)

Around 1793 there were many men in Europe; but of all, the consummate man was probably Captain Nelson. And what of Napoleon? you may ask. Napoleon, rather than a man, was a superman or demigod.

For the very reason that Nelson was so exclusively and enormously a man, he seems to have been many other things. A man who is a "measure of all things" is a crossroads of the Universe, and the starting point for roads leading everywhere. By extending his features, in one sense or another, one can achieve splendid and extraordinary images. Human fantasy is a dense atmosphere in which the phenomenon of the *Fata Morgana* is always produced. Thus, for the neoclassic provincial, abundant in that period, who read

the gazettes, Nelson was an Atlantic genius imposing
order upon the seas. Seen in this way, from a distance, Nelson was Neptune. The provincial man read
the gazette sitting before a fireplace upon which
stood a bronze clock; the dial of the clock was en-
cased in the round hollow of a metal wave, upon
which a floating naked god, with a trident in his
hand, was reclining. It was Nelson. But, seen from
close up, he was something else. He was many other
things: a small man with a hard expression, as tough
as the shell of a mollusk, and with the smoldering
spirit of an English triton. He was a being who does
not need poetry to live, but detests it and shakes it
off like dust from the road by day or the whirring
mosquitoes by night. (After living the best moments
of his life in Naples—moments of amorous fire upon
the already desert-like stretch of maturity—all that
occurs to him to say about Italy is that it is an intolerable country of violinists, poets, and scoundrels.)
His seafaring life is composed of violent gusts of wind
which pass over him and each time take something
away: first one limb, then another. Away with his
arm! Away with his eye! And the curious thing is that
each one of these amputations and losses emphasizes
more strongly how much of one piece this man was.
His courage became concentrated in the remaining
limbs.

Before conquering Bonaparte's fleet in Abukir, he
draws into the Bay of Naples one day with his big-

bellied frigates. He goes to the English embassy, where he is received by the ambassador, Sir William Hamilton.

Humanity is a vast, expansive concept: Admiral Nelson and Ambassador Hamilton can be placed at its opposite extremes, and one does not hinder the other.

We would like to have known this gentleman, to have been one of his friends, and to have had a talk with him. For Hamilton was a man of the world, a great collector and a great skeptic. The skeptic is the man with the fullest, richest, and most complete life. Some foolish idea leads us to suppose that the skeptic does not believe in anything. Quite the contrary! The skeptic differs from the dogmatic in that the latter believes in only one thing and the former in many, in almost everything. And this multitude of beliefs, acting as mutual restraints, make the mind flexible and prolific. Hamilton was one of the first to collect "classical" objects, and it is he who began the excavations of Pompey. His unequaled collection is now, I believe, in the British Museum.

Nelson is introduced to the ambassador's wife, and for the first time the triton feels gnawed at by an indefinable power. Here we have the fable in motion, a fundamental fable which all writers and philosophers have striven to avoid; I, too, of course. The fable is this: Nelson and Hamilton, the two most opposite male types that can be imagined, have fallen in love with the same Lady Hamilton. Naturally all the other intermediary types have also succumbed to her magic.

The fable is complete if we answer this question: Who is Lady Hamilton?

Lady Hamilton is that lady with the white plume, now galloping past us upon a bay steed. She is the intimate, over-intimate friend of the Neapolitan Queen María Carolina, the sister of Marie Antoinette, who has produced eighteen children and still has enough reserved vigor for her attachment to this Englishwoman. Emma Hamilton is the most beautiful lady in the United Kingdom, an "official beauty," whom people point out to each other from afar as if she were a national monument. She sings with a pleasing voice and at parties she assumes "poses". With a few shawls and dressed in the Greek manner, she poses as Clytemnestra or Cassandra. She wrinkles her brow tragically or makes her divine face appear melancholy, reflecting light slant-wise from her eyes, as do the figures of Guido Reni. Her triumph is enormous: these "poses" are spoken about all over Europe. Let it not be forgotten: we are about to enter the age of Romanticism. The heart is going to the head. Emotion is accepted as a sort of alcohol; it is a new inebriating taste, and people are now, more than anything else, seeking inebriation. The woman is about to serve as a subject or pretext for the exaltation of the sentiments. The tenor of the epoch is proclaimed in its vocabulary: at every mo-

ment you hear "divine," "sublime," "ecstatic," "fatal."
Tears and pearls are the fashion.

All this, when seen from afar, is appealing and attractive. The theater merges with life, and life puffs up and swells like a sail in the wind blowing from offstage. I do not know; but I think that this theatricality of life—which explains the romantic success of the "poses" executed by Emma Hamilton—is more admirable than the opposite principle, in force one hundred years later, when the theater is preoccupied with imitating life.

Now this Emma, the friend of the Queen, the Ambassador's wife, and Lady Hamilton, who was she before? She was the mistress of Hamilton's nephew, Grenville, who passed her on to his uncle. He had met her at the home of a healer who, by means of electric shocks, restored vitality to decrepit men. Standing before the healing sofa on which the patient received the shocks, this marvelous girl, who had been humbly raised and born of a cook, posed as "Hygeia," or "Health." Now she is the wife of the Ambassador of England. It is not easy to rise from the depths to the heights.

"Beauty is not enough," the reader will say, "to explain such a glorious ascent. This woman must have had a great talent."

For me this is the decisive point of the fable, the one we all usually avoid. The plain truth is that Lady Hamilton had neither talent nor even a fine upbringing and scarcely any taste or good judgment. She is the perfect feather-brain. Living for her is putting on and taking off dresses, coming and going from one party to another party. Spending money. Never standing still. Dances, little gestures, inviting and being invited. She is the eternal worldly woman who, in one form or another, we have all known and with whom almost all of us have fallen in love at some time. That is why I say that the fable is fundamental, and not a mere anecdote.

The reader, faced with this, turns around and says: "She must have been an extraordinary beauty." Yes, so it seems; but this does not explain, either, why men like Nelson and Hamilton fell in love with her so completely. Extraordinary beauty acts as an obstacle to men of fine sensibilities feeling attracted by a woman. The excessive perfection of a face encourages us to objectify its possessor and to keep at a distance from her in order to admire her as an aesthetic object. The only ones who fall in love with "official beauties" are fools and drugstore clerks. They are public monuments, curiosities which one views momentarily and from a distance. In their presence one feels like a tourist and not a lover.

It is advisable, then, for us not to evade the question by way of the avenue of beauty. If she had not possessed some degree of beauty, these two very different heroes—Nelson and Hamilton—would not have loved Emma; but what really attracted them was something else. I hope that the reader resists the plebeian and commonplace temptation to suppose that love in men of this rank springs from sexual appetite. But then we run into an enigma. . . .

Lady Hamilton, agile, sprightly, with an animated little head full of devious means, appears in the background of the landscape like a deer. This is the landscape which hangs in almost all the houses in England. Lady Hamilton does not have much more sense than a deer. Why do two men like Nelson and Hamilton fall in love with her?

The probable solution to the enigma is quite serious, and I do not know if I dare to promise it for the next number.

Olmedo's Solution

I have met Olmedo. Who is Olmedo? To my taste, an admirable man. He is intelligent, yet he is not an intellectual. I do not know if others have had the same experience; but from what I have seen of life I have the disturbing conviction that, at least in our time, there are no intelligent men other than intellectuals. And since the majority of intellectuals are not intelligent either, it turns out that intelligence is an exceedingly rare event on this planet. This conviction, the pronouncement of which will probably, and justly so, irritate the reader, is also extremely painful and upsetting for the one who holds it. This is true for many reasons, but especially because, taking it as a point of departure, it becomes enormously probable that one's own self is not at all intelligent and, consequently, that all of one's ideas are false (including this one which judges intelligence to be a rare occurrence). But it is unavoidable. No one can jump outside of his shadow nor have convictions other than those he has. All that one can ask is that each one sing his song with fidelity. And my present song could bear the same title as Massillon's famous sermon, *sur le petit nombre des élus*. Nothing has instilled more melancholy in me than the discovery that the number of intelligent men is extremely small.

I am not seeking genius in the next man. By intelligence I mean only that the mind react to happenings with a certain sharpness and precision, that the radish not be perpetually seized by its leaves, that the gray not be confused with brown and, above all, that objects in front of one be seen with a little exactness and accuracy, without supplanting sight by mechanically repeated words. But, ordinarily, one has the impression of living amid somnambulists who advance through life buried in an hermetic sleep from which it is impossible to stir them in order to make them aware of their surroundings. Probably, humanity has almost always lived in this somnambulistic state in which ideas are not a wide-awake, conscious reaction to things, but a blind, automatic habit, drawn from a repertory of formulae which the atmosphere infuses into the individual.

It is undeniable that a large part of science and literature has also been produced in a somnambulistic trance; that is to say, by creatures who are not at all intelligent. Science, particularly in our day, at once specialized and systematized, permits the utilization of the fool, so that we constantly see undistinguished people performing admirable work. Science and literature, as such, do not imply perspicacity; but, undoubtedly, their cultivation is a stimulant which favors the awakening of the mind and preserves it in that luminous state of alertness which constitutes intelligence. The difference between the intelligent man and the fool is, after all, that the former lives on guard against his own foolishness, recognizes it as soon as it appears, and strives to eliminate it, whereas the fool enchantedly surrenders to his foolishness without reservations.

Due to the fact of a constant stimulus, there is a greater probability that an intellectual will be intelligent; but I consider it a grave misfortune if, in any period or nation, intelligence remains, practically speaking, reduced to the limits of the intellectual. Intelligence asserts itself above all not in art, nor in science, but in intuition of life. The intellectual, however, barely lives; he is usually a man with poverty of intuition; his acts in the world are few and he has very little knowledge of women, business, pleasure, and passion. He leads an abstract existence, and can rarely throw a morsel of authentic live meat to the sharp-pointed teeth of his intellect.

The intellectual's intelligence is of very little use to us: it almost always acts upon unreal subjects, matters of his own profession. It is, therefore, a delight for me to meet Olmedo, to see him arrive smiling, preceded by the double-edged foil of his glance—a penetrating and almost cynical glance, which seems to lift the skirts of everything to see what it is like underneath. Olmedo is a banker and a man of the great world. When he passes rapidly through my squalid intellectual existence, he seems to me to be a glittering meteorite arriving laden with golden sidereal dust. Wherever he comes from, I know that he is always coming from the universe, and that during his journey he has caught a side glance of what was happening in Venus and has given Neptune a pat on the backside. Olmedo knows a great deal about books; he knows as much as the intellectual; but he knows it, not as an intellectual, but as a man of the world. He has never permitted the axis of his being to remain fixed and thereby limited to any profession, but he lets it wander in the drift of his uni-personal destiny. In other periods—for example, in the eighteenth century—there must have been many men like this: noblemen, financiers, property-holders, magistrates, who were, nevertheless, intelligent and who took pleasure in distilling clear, individual ideas out of their vital experiences. (The present situation in Europe—its incapacity to resolve gracefully the problems before it—can only be explained if one supposes that today men of this class are lacking. Thus as there are periods, *verbi gratia,* the end of Roman history, in which bravery becomes so rare that finally no one is brave other than military men, so there are other periods in which intelligence becomes restricted to intellectuals and hence a profession.)

A great deal is said about Olmedo in a yet unpublished (perhaps never to be published) history in which certain aspects of present-day life in Madrid are described with disturbing accuracy.

"I just saw your article on Lady Hamilton," Olmedo said to me. "You did very well to stress the essential paradigm in the situation; but now, out with the solution to the problem!"

"The fact is, my friend Olmedo, that I don't have the solution."

"Are you saying this seriously?"

"Completely seriously!"

"Then you are the bourgeois gentleman of psychology."

"Why?"

"Because you resolve problems without knowing it."

"How's that?"

"In stating the problem you actually give the solution. After all, it almost always happens that way. Our enigmas and questions are usually disguised answers with the false curlicues of question marks. That is what is happening now. Nelson and Hamilton, two men of opposite but first-class temperaments, fall in love with a woman who, by her graceful charm and her lack of sense, turns out to be more or less a deer. Here is the problem, you say."

"In fact. . . ."

"However, I do not see any problem here; rather, a fact as clear and perfect as a mathematical equation. You are the one who adds the problem because you approach so clear a fact with a preconceived idea, which is this: worthwhile men do not fall in love with deer."

"It seems natural that a man with a complex, disciplined mind could not feel attracted by a flighty, fickleminded creature who is, as one of Baroja's characters says, 'without substance'!"

"Yes, yes; it seems natural; but what is natural is not what appears so to us, but what appears so to Nature, who is much more natural than all our mental symmetries and has much more sense. After all, what reason is there for an intelligent man to fall in love with an intelligent woman? If one is trying to establish a business, a political party, or a scientific school, it is understandable that a clear mind will try to link itself to other clear minds; but the need for love— even leaving aside its sexual dimension—has nothing to do with these things; it is precisely the opposite of all rational preoccupations. Far from being an enigma, the situation you present is the key to amorous experience. Men fall in love with deer, with what there is of the deer in a woman. I would not say this in front of the ladies, because they would feign great anger, although deep down nothing could flatter them more."

"Then, for you, a woman's talent, her capacity for

sacrifice, her nobility, are unimportant qualities . . . ?"

"No, no; they are very important, they are won-
derful, most admirable—we look for them and exalt
them in the mother, the wife, the sister, the daughter.
When it's a question, however, strictly speaking, of
falling in love, one falls in love with the hidden deer
which lies in a woman."

"What the deuce are you saying?"

"The more of a man one is, the more is he filled to
the brim with rationality. Everything he does and
achieves he does and achieves for a reason, especially for a practical reason. A woman's love, that
divine surrender of her ultra-inner being which the
impassioned woman makes, is perhaps the only thing
which is not achieved by reasoning. The core of the
feminine mind, no matter how intelligent the woman
may be, is occupied by an irrational power. If the
male is the rational being, the female is the irrational
being. And that is the supreme delight which we find
in her! The animal is also irrational, but it is not a person; it is incapable of self-awareness and of respond-
ing to us, of being aware of us. There is no room for
relating or being intimate with it. The woman offers
the man the magic opportunity of relating with another being *without reasoning,* of influencing, dominating, surrendering to another, without any reason
entering into it. Believe me: if birds had the minimum personality necessary for being able to respond
to us, we would all fall in love with birds and not

with women. And, vice versa, if the normal male does not fall in love with another male, it is because he sees that the other man's mind is made up completely of rationality, logic, mathematics, poetry, business, and economy. What, from a masculine point of view, we call absurd and a woman's whim is precisely what attracts us. The world is admirably made by an excellent supervisor, and all of its parts are assembled and adjusted like a charm!"

"You are stupefying, Olmedo, my friend!"

"The idea, then, that the worthwhile man has to fall in love with a worthwhile woman, in the rational sense, is pure geometry. The intelligent man feels a slight revulsion for the very talented woman, unless her over-rationality is compensated for by over-irrationality. The over-rational in a woman smacks of masculinity and, rather than love, he feels friendship and admiration for her. It is just as false to assume that the eminent man attracts the "very clever" woman as it is to embrace the other idea that women propagate without involvement and, therefore, above all, seek beauty in a man. The ugly, but intelligent, man knows very well that, finally, he must cure women of the boredom contracted in their love affairs with handsome men. One after another, he sees them forced to rebound, infinitely fed up with their sally through the landscape of masculine beauty."

"Olmedo, my friend, if you were a writer and wrote all this that you're telling me, they'd hang you from a lamppost . . ."

"That is why I don't write. Why write? It is impossible to instil in others what is obvious to oneself. It is very rare for someone to attempt sympathetically to understand us exactly. But, after all, what I am saying was already said in substance many years ago, by our friend *Fede*. [Olmedo calls Friedrich Nietzsche *Fede*.] Where he enumerates the characteristic traits of the superior man, whom he calls the 'distinguished man', we find this:

Complacency is in women as in beings of a lesser, perhaps, but finer and lighter species. What a delight to encounter creatures who have their heads always filled with dancing and whims and clothes! They are the charm of all over-tense and serious masculine souls, whose life is filled with enormous responsibilities."

portrait of
Salome

In the morphology of the female there are perhaps no stranger figures than Judith and Salome, the two women who possess two heads apiece: their own and a severed one.

It is curious that in every existent species extreme cases appear in which the species seems to negate itself and convert into its reverse. They are borderline types which, so to speak, belong to overlapping kingdoms, like certain animals which are almost plants, or certain chemical substances which are almost living plasma. There lies in them the ambiguity typical of all that is terminal and extreme; thus, one is ignorant of whether the profile of their bodies, which defines their line of circumscription, belongs to them or to the surrounding space which limits them.

A serious study, not bogged down in anecdotes or in a casuistry of chance, would reveal to us that the essence of femininity exists in the fact that an individual feels her destiny totally fulfilled when she surrenders herself to another individual. Everything else that the woman does or is has an adjectival and derivative character. In opposition to this marvelous phenomenon, masculinity presents the deep-rooted instinct which impels it to take possession of another person. There exists, therefore, a pre-established harmony between woman and man; for the former, living means surrender; for the latter, living means taking possession; and both destinies, precisely because they are opposites, come to a perfect agreement.

It is an error to assume that the specific man and the specific woman will always conform purely and completely to this pattern; in fact conflict arises when deviations and interferences occur in the deep-rooted instincts of masculinity and femininity. The classification of human beings into men and women is, obviously, inexact; reality presents innumerable gradations between both extremes. Biology demonstrates how physical sexuality hovers indecisively over the embryo to the point that it is possible to subject it experimentally to a change of sex. Each existing individual represents a peculiar equation in which both genders participate, and nothing is more infrequent than to find someone who is "all man" or "all woman." What occurs in physical sexuality becomes even more noticeable when we observe psychological sexuality. According to the masculine and feminine principle, the *Yin* and the *Yang* of Chinese tradition, both spirits seem to struggle with each other and arrive at different forms of compromise, which are the various types of man and woman.

Thus, Judith and Salome are two variations of that type of woman which is most surprising because it is the most contradictory: the woman of prey.

It would be a vain effort to attempt to speak adequately about either figure without due length; therefore, I shall limit myself at this time to presenting a very brief portrayal of Salome.

The growth of a Salome occurs only at the summit of society. In Palestine she was a pampered, idle princess, and today she could be the daughter of a banker or an oil king. The decisive factor is that her upbringing, in an atmosphere of potency, erased in her mind the dynamic line which separates the real from the imaginary. All of her desires were satisfied, and what was undesirable was eliminated from her environment. The essential fact of her legend, the key to her psychological mechanism, is that Salome got whatever she wanted. Since desiring something meant for her getting it, all of the operations which the rest of us generally have to perform in order to achieve a realization of our appetites remained atrophied within her. Her energies, unoccupied as they were, were channeled into a turbine of desire, transforming Salome into a prodigious mass of desires and fantasies. This, at once, signifies a deformation of femininity. Normally a woman imagines and fantasizes less than a man, and this accounts for her more flexible adaptation to the real destiny imposed upon her. The things which a male desires are usually creations of his imagination and independent of reality; the woman, on the contrary, wants something which she discovers among real things. Likewise, in the erotic realm: it is frequent for the man to invent *a priori*, like Chateaubriand, a *fantôme d'amour*, an unreal image of a woman to which he dedicates his passion. It is not by chance that this is exceedingly uncommon in the woman, because poverty of imagination characterizes the feminine psyche.

Salome fantasizes in a masculine manner. Since her imaginary life is the most real and vivid part of her experience, femininity incurs a masculine deviation. Let one add to this the persistence with which legend alludes to her unviolated virginity, and it becomes clear how, in a woman, extreme physical virginity, an immoderate preoccupation with prolonging the state of maidenhood, usually appears in conjunction with a masculine nature. Mallarmé perceived the situation quite accurately when he supposed that Salome was frigid. Her flesh, firm and flexible, with fine acrobatic muscles—Salome was a dancer—covered with the glitter of her gems and precious metals, gave the impression, when in movement, of an "inviolate reptile."

Salome would not have been a woman if she had not felt compelled to surrender her person to another; but, imaginative and frigid woman that she was, she surrendered to a vision, a daydream of her own making. In this manner, her femininity found complete expression in an imaginary dimension. In regard to her amorous chimera, however, Salome finally discovered the distance between the fantastic and the real. The powerful tetrarch could not create a man to coincide with the image housed in that audacious little head. The situation inevitably repeats itself; every Salome, raised in the midst of opulence, leads a life which is ill-humored, unpleasant, and, basically, suffused with bitterness. Lacking an actual figure upon whom to fasten her phantasmagoric creations, she tries, like someone fitting dresses on a manikin, to attach the unreal lines of her daydream to the men who pass before her.

For reasons that presently elude us, Salome came one day to believe that she had found the embodiment of her vision on earth. Perhaps it is merely a question of a *quid pro quo*: the coincidence of her paradigm with this man of flesh and bone named John the Baptist was more negative than anything else. His only resemblance to her ideal was that he was different from other men. Salome always looks for a man who is so different from other men that he seems almost to belong to an unknown sex; another sign of deformed femininity. The Baptist was a hairy, frenzied character who shouted in the desert and preached a hydrotherapeutic religion. Salome could not have done worse; John the Baptist was a man of ideas, a *homo religiosus*, the opposite pole of Don Juan, who is the *homme à femmes*.

The tragedy inevitably explodes, like a chemical reaction.

Salome loved her vision; it was to this, not to John the Baptist, that she had surrendered. The latter was merely the occasion for giving embodiment to the former. Salome's feeling for her hirsute man was not one of love, but rather the hunger to be loved by him. Salome's masculinity inescapably had to lead her into a sexual relationship in which she assumed the masculine attitude.

A man feels love primarily as a violent desire to be loved, whereas for a woman the primary experience is to feel love itself, the warm flow which radiates from her being toward her beloved and the impulse toward him. The need to be loved is felt by her only consequently and secondarily. The normal woman is the opposite of the beast, who pounces on his prey. She is the prey who pounces on the beast.

Salome, who does not love John the Baptist, nevertheless needs to be loved by him. She needs to take possession of his person, and in order to carry out this masculine desire she will employ all sorts of violence which normally the male uses to impose his will upon the environment. That is why, just as other women carry a lily in their hands, this woman carries a dismembered head in her marble-like fingers. It is her vital prey. With a rhythmic step, a swaying torso, a rooklike Hebrew face, she advances through the legend, and above her rigid head, with glassy eyes, her mien leans forward with the rapacious curve of a goshawk or falcon . . .

In all events, the tragic flirtation between Salome, the princess, and John the Baptist, the intellectual, is too intricate and drawn-out a story for me to tell now.

toward a psychology of
                    the interesting man

1

Nothing is so flattering to a man as to hear women say that he is interesting. But when is a man interesting in the opinion of a woman? This is one of the most subtle and difficult questions to raise. In order to tackle it systematically, an entirely new and heretofore unattempted discipline would have to be developed, one which I have considered and reconsidered for years. I call it *Knowledge of Man* or *Philosophical Anthropology*. This discipline will reveal to us that souls, like bodies, have different forms. With varying degrees of clarity, depending upon individual insight, we all perceive this diversity of personality structure in the people whom we encounter. It is difficult, nevertheless, to transform our surface perceptions into clear concepts, into complete knowledge. We sense others, but we do not know them.

Everyday language has accumulated, however, a wealth of delicate insights which are conveyed by highly suggestive verbal capsules. One speaks, in fact, of hardy souls and gentle souls, of souls which are dour or sweet, profound or superficial, strong or weak, plodding or flighty. One speaks of magnanimous and pusillanimous men, thus recognizing stature in souls as well as bodies. One says of someone that he is a man of action or on the other hand that he is a contemplative man, that he is "cerebral" or sentimental, etc. No one has attempted to analyze methodically the precise meaning of the many different designations under which we classify the marvelous diversity of the human *fauna.* All these expressions merely allude to the structural differences of the inner person, and point toward constructing a psychological anatomy. It is clear that a boy's soul will of necessity have a different structure from an old man's, and an ambitious man a different spiritual make-up from a dreamer. This study, if undertaken somewhat systematically, might result in a new-styled, cogent charactery, which would permit us to describe with hitherto unsuspected refinement the varieties of human inwardness. Among them might appear what, according to women, is the *interesting man.*

To enter upon a thorough analysis of the interesting man fills me with fear, since we face thereupon a maze of problems. The first and most obvious thing to be said about the interesting man is this: the interesting man is the man with whom women fall in love. But this immediately leads us astray, and plunges us into greater perils. We are thrust straight into the jungle of love. And the fact is that no land in human topography is less explored than love. It could in fact be said that everything remains to be said of love; or rather, that everything remains to be thought about it.

A store of crude ideas fixed in people's heads prevents them from seeing the facts with normal clarity. Everything is confused and distorted. There are many reasons for this. In the first place, love, by nature, is part of one's secret life. One cannot tell about one's love; in the telling it vanishes or vaporizes. Everyone has to rely upon his personal experience, almost always meager, for it is not easy to profit from that of one's neighbor. What would have happened, however, to physics if each physicist possessed only his personal observations? In the second place, what happens is that the men who are most capable of thinking about love are the ones who have experienced it the least, whereas those who have experienced it are usually incapable of thinking about it, of subtly analyzing its iridescent and ever-vague plumage. Finally, an experiment on love is a most thankless task. If a doctor talks about digestion, people listen modestly and curiously. But if a psychologist speaks about love, everyone listens to him disparagingly, or they do not listen to him at all; they never even bother to find out what he has to say, because they all believe themselves to be experts on the subject. In few instances does the habitual stupidity of people appear so manifestly. They act as though love were not, after all, as theoretical a subject as others, hermetically sealed away from anyone who approaches it with inadequate intellectual tools!

It is the same as with the subject of Don Juan. Everyone thinks he has the true interpretation of Don Juanism, that most obscure, abstruse, delicate problem of our time. The fact is that, with few exceptions, men can be divided into three classes: those who think they are Don Juan, those who think they have been Don Juan, and those who think they could have been Don Juan but did not want to be. The last are the ones who propose, with worthy intention, to attack Don Juan, and perhaps decree his dismissal.

There exist, then, numerous reasons why the sciences which everyone presumes to understand—love and politics—are the ones which have progressed least. Those who are best qualified to speak about love and politics have kept silent simply to avoid listening to the clichés which ignorant people hasten to utter as soon as either subject is touched upon.

It ought to be made clear, therefore, that neither the Don Juans nor those in love know anything in particular about Don Juan or love. Probably the only person who can speak with precision on both matters is he who lives at a distance from both, but is yet, like the astronomer in regard to the sun, attentive and curious. Knowing things is not being them, nor being them knowing them. In order to see an object it is necessary to be detached from it. Separation converts it from experienced reality into an object of knowledge. Any other view would lead us, for example, to believe that the zoologist, in order to study ostriches, must himself become an ostrich; which is exactly what Don Juan becomes when he speaks about himself.

For my part, I can say that I have not attained sufficient clarity on this important matter, in spite of having thought about it a great deal. Fortunately, Don Juan is not under discussion now. What should be said, perhaps, is that Don Juan is always an interesting man, contrary to what his enemies wish to make us believe. It is evident, however, that not every interesting man is a Don Juan—and with this comment on him let us eliminate his dangerous profile from these notes. As for love, it will be less easy to avoid its intrusion into our purview. I find myself, therefore, forced to formulate with apparent dogmatism, without development or proof, some of my thoughts about love which differ radically from accepted ideas. The reader ought to take them merely as a necessary clarification of what I have to say about the *interesting man* and not insist, for the moment, on deciding whether or not they are correct.

2

As I suggested before, the first thing which ought to be said about the interesting man is that he is the man with whom women fall in love. But, one may immediately object that all normal men find love in some woman, and, consequently, all must be interesting. To which I must peremptorily give two answers. First: not one woman, but many, fall in love with the interesting man. The "all" and the "nothing," the "many" and the "none" should be understood as oversimplifications which do not aim at exactness. Exactness in dealing with every problem of life would be most inexact, and quantitative judgments are made rather to express typical situations, norms, tendencies.

The belief that love is a dull and banal affair is one of the greatest impediments in the way of understanding the erotic phenomena. This view results from a common confusion: with the single noun *love* we designate the most diverse psychological states. For this reason our concepts and generalizations never concur with reality. What holds true for love in one meaning of the word does not hold for another, and our observation, perhaps valid in the area of eroticism where it was made, turns out to be false when extended to others.

The origin of this confusion is clear. All manner of attractions between man and woman are manifested, broadly speaking, in a limited range of social and private behavior. The man who likes a woman's body; the man who is attracted to her out of vanity; the man who goes out of his mind as a victim of the ignoble effect a woman can produce with a skillful tactic of attraction and disdain; the man who simply sticks to a woman out of tenderness, loyalty, sympathy, "affection"; the man who falls into a state of passion; and, finally, the man who is truly in love, behave in a more or less identical manner. If someone observes their actions from afar, he does not notice the subtle qualifications of "more or less." By paying attention only to the broad pattern of behavior he judges that there is nothing different about it, and, therefore, decides that there is nothing distinctive about the sentiment which inspires it either. But all he would have to do is to take a magnifying glass and study them close up to see that only the general pattern of actions is alike, and that there are among them the most diverse variations. It is an enormous error to analyze a love affair by its actions and words. Generally neither the one nor the other reflects love but, rather, they constitute a repertoire of grand gestures, rites, and formulae, created by society, which sentiment finds at its disposal, like a piece of available equipment thrust upon it and which it finds itself obliged to use. It is only the small original gesture, the tone, and the most subtle signs of behavior which allow us to differentiate between the various kinds of love.

I speak now only of true romantic love, which is radically different from sensual ardor, *amour-vanité*, ignoble involvements, "affection," and "passion." Here is a varied amorous *fauna* whose multiform composition could well be categorized.

Romantic love—which is, in my opinion, the prototype and summit of all eroticisms—is characterized by its simultaneously possessing these two ingredients: a feeling of being "enchanted" by another being who produces complete "illusion" in us, and a feeling of being absorbed by him to the core of our being, as if he had torn us from our own vital depths and we were living transplanted, our vital roots within him. Another way of saying this is that a person in love feels himself totally surrendered to the one he loves; so that it does not matter whether bodily or spiritual surrender has actually taken place. It is possible for a person in love to succeed in preventing, by virtue of reflective considerations,— social decorum, difficulties of any nature—the surrender of his will to the one he loves. What is essential is that he *feels* himself, regardless of the decision of his will, surrendered to the other.

There is no contradiction in this, because the fundamental surrender is not carried out on the plane of will, but occurs more deeply within the person. There is no will to surrender: there is an unwilled surrender. And regardless of where our will leads us, we remain unwittingly surrendered to the beloved, even if we are led to the other end of the world to be away from him.[1]

This extreme case of disassociation, of antagonism between will and love, serves to emphasize the peculiarity of the latter, and should be taken into account as a possible complication—*possible,* but certainly quite improbable. Considerations of self-defense against the beloved rarely influence the will of a person genuinely in love. This is true to such a point that if, in practice, one sees that the beloved's will is active, that he "presents considerations," and finds "very respectable" reasons for not loving or for loving less, it is usually the surest sign that, actually, he is not in love. Such a soul feels itself vaguely attracted by the other but has not been uprooted from itself—which is only to say that this man is not in love.

The combination of these two elements, enchantment and surrender, is, then, essential to the love which we are discussing. This combination is no accident. Both do not merely chance to co-exist, but rather one is born out of and takes nourishment from the other. What exists in love is surrender due to enchantment.

A mother surrenders to her child, a friend to his friend, but not because of "illusion" or "enchant-

[1] In my essay *Vitalidad, Alma, Espíritu,* the psychological foundation of this difference between soul and will can be seen (The Spectator. V).

ment." The mother does so out of a deep-rooted instinct which has almost nothing to do with her spirituality. The friend surrenders by a clear decision of his will. He possesses loyalty, which by its very nature is a reflective virtue. We might say that the friend takes himself in his own hand and offers himself to another. What is true of love, however, is that our soul escapes from our hand and is sucked in by the other. This suction which another personality exercises upon one's life sustains the latter in a state of levitation, uproots it from its own being and transplants it to the beloved, where the original roots seem to take root again, as in new soil. Thanks to this a person in love lives not off himself but off the other, as a child, before birth, lives bodily off its mother, in whose womb it is planted and immersed.

This absorption of the lover by the beloved is simply the effect of enchantment. Another being enchants us, and we feel this enchantment in the form of a continual, gently elastic pull from within. The much overworked word "enchantment" is the one, nevertheless, which best expresses the type of attraction which the beloved exercises upon the lover. Its use ought to be restored by resuscitating the connotation of magic which it originally possessed.

In sexual attraction there is no real attraction. A suggestive body excites one's appetite, one's desire for it. However, our desire does not lead toward the desired object but, on the contrary, our soul pulls away from the desired object toward itself. That is why it is very accurate to say that the object *awakens* a desire, as if to indicate that it does not participate in the process of desiring itself, but rather that its role ends when it stimulates desire, leaving us to do the rest. The psychological phenomenon of desire and that of "being enchanted" produce reverse reactions. In the first, the object tends to be absorbed, while in the second the "I" is absorbed. Appetite, therefore, does not result in surrender of oneself, but, on the contrary, in the capture of the object.[2]

Equally, there is no real surrender in "passion." Lately this inferior form of love has achieved undeserved merit and favor. Some think that the measure of one's love is in proportion to one's proximity to the suicide or murder of Werther or Othello, and

---

[2] This old term "appetite" encompasses an error in psychological description, which, however, is very common. It confuses the psychic phenomenon which it is trying to classify with the consequences incurred. Because I want something, I try to move toward it, in order to *take it*. This "moving toward"—*petere*—is the means which desire finds to satisfy itself, but it is not desire itself. On the other hand, the final act, the capture of the object, the bringing of it toward myself, the embracing of the object within myself, is the original manifestation of desire.

The habit of confusing love with its consequences has also obscured the description of love. The amorous sentiment, the most fertile in the life of the psyche, spawns innumerable acts which accompany it like the followers of a Roman patrician. Thus, desire toward the beloved is always born of love; but these desires are not love. On the contrary, they presuppose love because they arise from it.

the insinuation is that every other form of love is imaginary and "cerebral." I think that, on the contrary, the term "passion" should be restored to its ancient pejorative meaning. Turning a revolver on oneself or on another does not guarantee in the slightest the quality or even the quantity of a sentiment. "Passion" is a pathological state which implies defectiveness of soul. A person vulnerable to the mechanism of obsession, or one possessing a very simple, crude nature will turn every germ of feeling that befalls him into "passion," that is, mania.[3] Let us tear down the romantic trappings that have adorned passion. Let us cease believing that the measure of a man's love lies in how stupid he has become or is willing to be.

Far from it: it would be well to establish the following aphorism as a general principle in the psychology of love: *since love is the most delicate and total act of a soul, it will reflect the state and nature of the soul. The characteristics of the person in love must be attributed to love itself.* If the individual is not sensitive, how can his love be sentient? If he is not profound, how can his love be deep? As one is, so is his love. For this reason, *we can find in love the most decisive symptom of what a person is.* All other acts and appearances can deceive us with regard to his true nature, but his love affairs reveal to

[3] The man who kills or kills himself because of love would do it equally for any other cause: a dispute, a loss of fortune, etc.

us the carefully concealed secret of his being. This is especially true in the choice of the beloved. In no other action do we reveal our innermost character as we do in erotic choice.

Frequently we hear that intelligent women fall in love with stupid men, and vice versa, foolish women with clever men. I confess that although I have heard this many times, I have never believed it, and in every case in which I was able to draw closer and apply the psychological magnifying lens, I have found either that those men and women were not actually intelligent or that their chosen ones were not stupid.

Passion is not, therefore, the height of amorous feeling but, on the contrary, its degeneration in inferior souls. In it there is not—or, at least there does not have to be—either enchantment or surrender. Psychiatrists know that the obsessed man struggles against his obsession, that he does not accept it, but yet is dominated by it. Thus there can be great passion with very little love. This will indicate to the reader that my interpretation of the amorous phenomenon is in direct opposition to the false mythology which makes of passion an elemental, primitive force engendered in the obscure bosom of human animality which brutally overpowers the person and ignores any appreciable role of loftier, more subtle portions of the soul.

Ignoring for the present the possible connection between love and certain cosmic instincts latent in our being, I think that love is indeed the complete opposite of an elemental force. I would say—aware though I am of the margin of error—that love, rather than being an elemental force, almost resembles a literary genre. This is a formula which—naturally—will provoke more than one reader before he considers it. Certainly, if this claimed to be the final word, it would be excessive and unacceptable. All that I wish to suggest, however, is that love is not an instinct but rather a creation, and, in man, no primitive creation at that. The savage has no inkling of it, the Chinese and the Indian are unfamiliar with it, the Greeks of the time of Pericles barely recognized it.[4] Could not both features—that of being a spiritual creation and that of appearing only in certain stages and forms of human culture—serve well as the definition of a literary genre?

[4] Plato had a perfect awareness of this sentiment and described it wonderfully, but it would never have occurred to him to confuse it with what a Greek of his time felt toward a woman. Love, in Plato, is romantic love in perhaps its first appearance in history. But it is the love of the mature, more cultivated man for the beautiful, discreet young man. Plato, without hesitation, sees in this love a privilege of Greek culture, a spiritual invention, and, in addition, a central institution of the new human life. We are revolted by this Doric way of love and with good reason, but pure truth obliges us to recognize in it one of the historic roots of this admirable Western invention of love for a woman. If the reader thinks for a while he will note that this is more complex and subtle than the common man thinks, and the comparison between love and a literary genre will seem less fantastic.

Love can be as clearly distinguished from its other pseudomorphs as from sensual ardor and "passion." This includes what I have called "affection." In "affection"—which, at best, is usually the form of matrimonial love—two people feel mutual sympathy, fidelity, adhesion, but there is no enchantment and surrender. Each lives absorbed in himself, without rapture in the other, and each emits from within himself gentle rays of consideration, benevolence, corroboration.

What has been said is sufficient to give some meaning—that is all I am attempting now—to this affirmation: if one wishes to see clearly into the phenomenon of love, it is necessary, above all, to free oneself from the common idea which sees it as a universal sentiment, within the reach of almost everyone's experience, occurring at every minute everywhere, regardless of the society, race, nationality or period in which we live. The features which the preceding pages outline reduce considerably the frequency of love, by removing many things from its sphere which are erroneously included. One final step and we may say without undue exaggeration that *love is an infrequent occurrence, a sentiment which only certain souls can hope to experience: in fact, a specific talent which some individuals possess, ordinarily granted in conjunction with other talents but which may occur alone.* Truly, falling in love is a marvelous talent which some creatures possess, like the gift of composing verses, the spirit of sacrifice, melodic inspiration, personal bravery, like knowing how to take command. Not everyone falls in love, nor do those capable of falling in love fall in love with just anyone. The divine event occurs only when certain rigorous conditions are present both in the subject and in the object. Very few can be lovers, and very few beloved. Love has its *ratio,* its law, its never-changing unitarian essence, which does not exclude from its exergue abundant casuistic distinctions and variability.[5]

3

All one has to do is to enumerate some of the conditions and assumptions of being in love to make its extreme infrequency obvious and plain. Without

[5] There exists today a group of men, among whom I am proud to find myself, that opposes the empirical tradition, according to which everything happens by chance and without any unified form, changing from time to time and place to place, making it unnecessary to find any law of events other than the "more or less" of statistical induction. In opposition to such vast anarchy we renew the older and more profound tradition of philosophy which seeks in all things the "essence," the single mode.

Clearly, it would be much more simple and convenient to think that love has infinite forms, that it is different in each case, etc. I hope always to remain aloof from the intellectual abasement which elicits this way of thinking and flatters inert minds so greatly. The ultimate mission of the intellect will always be to search for the "essence," that is to say, the unique mode of being of each reality.

claiming to be final, we could say that these conditions form three classes, since there are three components of love: *perception,* in order to see the person who is going to be loved; *emotion,* with which we respond sentimentally to the vision of what is beloved; and the *constitution* of our being, the nature of the soul in its totality. Although perception and emotion may function properly, it is impossible for love to uproot, invade, or mold our character if the constitution of our soul is insubstantial and inflexible, dispersed or without vigorous resources.

In order to be enchanted we must be, above all, capable of *seeing* another person—simply opening one's eyes will not do.[6] One needs a peculiar kind of initial curiosity which is much more integral, deep-rooted and broad than mere curiosity about things (like scientific, technical, or tourist curiosity, or curiosity to "see the world," etc.), or even about the particular acts of people (for example, gossip). One must be vitally curious about humanity, and more concretely, about the individual as a living totality, an individual *modus* of existence. Without this curiosity, the most eminent creatures can pass before us

[6] On this great enigma of how we see another person, I refer to two essays of mine: *"La Percepción del Prójimo"* (in *Teoría de Andalucía,* 2nd ed., 1944, p. 81) and *"Sobre la expresión, fenómeno cósmico"* (in *El Espectador,* VII).

and make no impression upon us. The ever-lit lamp of the evangelical virgins is the symbol of this virtue which constitutes, as it were, the threshold of love.

But note that such curiosity, in truth, presupposes many other things. It is a vital luxury which only organisms with a high level of vitality can possess. The weak individual is incapable of disinterested, initial attention to what occurs outside of himself. He fears the unexpected which life may hold enveloped in the folds of its billowing skirt, and he becomes hermetic to the extent that he does not immediately relate to others with total interest. This paradox of "disinterested" interest permeates love in all its functions and actions like the red mark which is stamped on all cables from the Royal English Navy.

Simmel—following Nietzsche—has said that the essence of life consists precisely in longing for more life. Living is to live even more, a desire to increase one's own palpitations. When it is not this, life is sick and, in its measure, is not life. The ability to interest oneself in a thing for what it is in itself and not in view of the profit which it will render us is the magnificent gift of generosity which flourishes only at the peaks of the greatest altitudes of vitality. A body weak from a medical standpoint does not in itself indicate a deficiency in vitality, as, by contrast, a Herculean physique does not guarantee organic energy (this is very frequently true of athletes).

Almost all men and women live submerged in the sphere of their own interests (some, without doubt, beautiful and respectable), and are incapable of feeling the migratory urge toward what is outside themselves. Whether treated well or badly by the landscape that surrounds them, they live definitively satisfied with the line of their horizon and do not miss the vague possibilities which they might realize only at a cost. This limited range is incompatible with deep-seated curiosity, which is, finally, an untiring instinct for migration, a wild urge to depart from oneself to the other.[7]

That is why it is so difficult for the *petit bourgeois* and the *petite bourgeoise* to fall in love in an au-

---

[7] In every society, race, and period, the possibility of frequent love fails because one or another condition is deficient. In Spain you need seek no further to explain the rarity of the erotic event, for the very first assumption is lacking. There are extremely few Spaniards, especially Spanish women, endowed with curiosity, and it is difficult to find someone who feels a yearning to peer out at life, to see what it has to offer. It is curious to attend a "society" gathering in our country: the lack of animation in dialogue and gestures soon reveals that one is among slumbering people (biologists call the winter drowsiness of certain species *vita minima*). No demand is made of the passing hour, and nothing is expected of one another, nor, in general, of existence. From my point of view it is immoral for a being not to make the most intense effort every instant of his life.

thentic manner; for them, life consists in an insistence on what is known and habitual, an unshakable satisfaction with the same daily routine.

This curiosity, which is simultaneously an eagerness for life, can only be found in porous souls where free air—cosmic air charged with stardust—circulates, unconfined by any limiting wall. But curiosity is not enough to make us "see" the delicate, complex structure of a person. Curiosity predisposes the eye, but the vision must be discerning. And such discernment is indeed the prime talent and extraordinary endowment which acts as a component in love. It serves as a special intuition which permits us to gain an immediate intimate knowledge of other men, the nature of their souls in conjunction with the meaning expressed by their bodies. Thanks to this we can "discriminate" between people, appreciate their quality, their triviality or their excellence; in short, their degree of vital perfection. Do not think by this that I am trying to intellectualize the sentiment of love. Discernment has nothing to do with intelligence, and although its presence is more likely in clear-minded creatures, it can exist in solitude, like poetic talent which so often finds a home in almost imbecilic men. Actually, it is unlikely to be found except in persons endowed with some sharpness of intellect, but the degree of discernment does not depend upon the degree of intelligence. Thus it happens that this intuition is usually found to be relatively more frequent in women than in men, whereas intellectual endowment is to be found more often among men.[8]

Those who imagine love to be a half-magical, half-mechanical effect will oppose my assertion that discernment is one of its essential attributes. According to them, love always blossoms "without reason." It is illogical, anti-rational and, in fact, excludes all discernment. This is one of the central points where I find myself obliged to differ resolutely from accepted ideas.

We say that a thought is logical when it does not sprout up out of nowhere, but, on the contrary, when we see it grow and seek sustenance from another of our thoughts which is its *psychic source*. The classic example is *the conclusion*. Because we believe the premises, we accept the consequence: if the former are placed in doubt, the judgment of the consequence is suspended. We cease to believe in it. The *reason* is the base, the proof, the explanation, the *logos*, in sum, which gives rationality to the thought. But, at the same time, the thought is the psychological source which produces rationality, the real force which originates and maintains it in our spirit.

Love, although there may be nothing intellectual

---

[8] Every biological function—in contrast to physico-chemical phenomena—presents its anomalies near to its norm. So it is with love. When the other conditions for love prevail and discernment is insufficient or nonexistent, you have an example of sentimental pathology, of anomalous love.

about it, is like reasoning in that it does not spring up out of nowhere and, so to speak, *ex nihilo,* but has its psychic source in the qualities of the beloved. The presence of these engenders and nourishes love, or, to put it another way, no one loves without reason; whoever is in love has, all the while, a conviction that his love is justified. To love is, furthermore, "to believe" (to feel) that that which is loved is, in fact, lovable for itself, just as thinking is believing that things are, in reality, what we think they are. It is possible that in both cases we are mistaken, that neither that which is loved is what we feel it is, nor that which is real is what we think it is; but in any case we keep on loving and thinking as long as we have our conviction. The logical character of thought consists of this quality of feeling oneself justified and living precisely *from* one's justification, relying on it at every instant, corroborating it with the proof of one's reason. Leibniz expresses the same thing by saying that thought is not blind, but that it thinks a thing *because it sees* that it is as it thinks it. Equally, love loves, because it sees that the object is lovable. Thus the lover comes away with the inevitable attitude of love, the only possible one which he could assume, and he cannot understand why others do not feel likewise—the origin of jealousy, which to some extent is of the same nature as love.

Love is not, therefore, illogical or anti-rational. It is, undoubtedly, a-logical and irrational, since *logos* and *ratio* refer exclusively to relationship of concepts. But there is a broader use of the term "reason" which includes everything that is not blind, everything that has *nous* meaning.[9] In my opinion, all normal love makes sense, is well founded, and is, consequently, *logoide*.

I continually feel myself further and further estranged from the contemporary tendency to believe that things have no *nous* meaning, that they happen blindly, like the movement of atoms, which a devastating mechanism has elevated to the prototype of all reality.[10] For this reason I consider that in true love it is essential for there to be a moment of discernment, which reveals the character of the individual in which sentiment has found "reason" to sprout and blossom.

This discernment may be great or small; it may be vulgar or inspired. Although not the most important, this is one of the reasons which leads me to classify love as a talent *sui generis*, which admits of all gradations from imbecile to genius, but, like corporal vision and intelligence, is of course susceptible to error. That which is mechanical and blind never errs. Many instances of amorous anomaly can be reduced to confusions in the lover's perception of the beloved: an optical illusion or mirage no less

[9] Pertaining to the mind or intellect (Translator).

[10] Of course my reason for rejecting the limitless extension of mechanism is not because it is devastating but because it is false and, in addition, it is world-devastating.

strange or explicable than those which our eyes often commit, without causing us to call ourselves blind. Precisely because love makes mistakes at times—although much less frequently than is believed—we have to restore to it the attribute of vision, for, as Pascal wished: "Poets have no right to picture love as blind: its bandage must be pulled off and henceforth it must be given the use of its eyes."

JOSÉ ORTEGA Y GASSET

*José Ortega y Gasset was born in Madrid in 1883, and was
educated there and in German universities, returning to his
native city in 1910 to become a professor of metaphysics.
Ortega founded several reviews, the best known of which
was* LA REVISTA DE OCCIDENTE, *and he lectured widely.
He left Spain at the beginning of the civil war, living first
in France and then in Argentina. He returned to Spain
in 1949, and died there in October 1955. In addition to*
ON LOVE, *the following of his many works have been
published in English translation:* THE MODERN THEME, THE
REVOLT OF THE MASSES, INVERTEBRATE SPAIN, TOWARDS A
PHILOSOPHY OF HISTORY, THE MISSION OF THE UNIVERSITY,
CONCORD AND LIBERTY, THE DEHUMANIZATION OF ART AND
OTHER WRITINGS ON ART AND CULTURE, MAN AND PEOPLE,
and MAN AND CRISIS.